How to be a billionaire

3rd Edition

Tony Pow

Contents

Highlights

Why you invest

You need to learn about investing sooner or later in your life. You need to take some calculated risks.

Compare the returns of the following assets: cash, CDs, treasury bills, bonds, real estate and stocks. We start with the risk-free investments and end with the riskiest. It turns out that the average returns are in the opposite order. Cash and CDs are not risk-free as inflation eats our profits. For example, the real return is negative for the 2% return in a CD and a 3% inflation rate. In addition you have to pay taxes for the 'returns'. Our capitalist system punishes us for not taking risk.

There are two kinds of risk: blind risk and calculated risk. If you buy a stock due to a recommendation from a commentator on TV or a tip, most likely you are taking a blind risk. It would be the same in buying a house without thoroughly evaluating the house and its neighborhood. When you buy stocks with a proven strategy (i.e. when/what stocks to buy and when/what stocks to sell), you are taking a calculated risk. In the long run, stocks with calculated and educated risks are profitable.

Be a turtle investor by investing in value stocks and holding for longer time periods (a year or more). "Buy and Monitor" is better an approach than "Buy and Hold" as some could lose all the stock values such as in the failure of Enron.

For experienced investors, shorting, short-term trading and covered calls would make you good profits. Simple market timing would reduce your losses during market down turns. If you buy a market ETF and use my simple market timing, you should have beaten the market by a wide margin from 2000 to 2019.

With so many frauds and poor management, do not trust anyone with your investing. Do not buy investing instruments that are highly marketed such as annuity and term insurance.

If you are a handyman and do not mind to satisfy the constant requests of your tenants, buy real estate in growing areas could be very profitable in the long run. Take advantage of the tax laws such as investing in a 401K especially the part that is matched by your company and/or a Roth IRA.

Why you want to read this book

This book should improve your financial health substantially. There are about a million investment books. Why we need another one?

- This is a lengthy book covering most topics in investing. Most of my paperbacks are eligible for a free digital version from Amazon.

- I select proven ideas from more than 100 books besides my original ideas and experiences. I also include links to current articles that will bring more depth to the topic. It is not a novel or documenting the story of my life. All related chapters are grouped in a section for easy future reference. Some chapters are not easy to digest as they have a lot of pointers and some may require you to try them out yourself.

- A best seller was written by a young writer whose main income was from his books and none from his investing. His book is good for beginners or you want to brush up your English. Most of my incomes are from investing.

- Many popular books claiming the authors making millions. However, usually their techniques are hard to follow. Many admitted they had been bankrupted many times. Hence, their chance of bankrupting again is very high. Is bankruptcy fine with you? I cannot afford bankruptcy past and present. My techniques minimize risking my money.

- There are many popular books. They worked very well at one time and folks making millions following the advice. However, look at their recent performances of the last five years. Most of them cannot even beat the S&P 500 index.

- Check the recent mediocre performance of gurus such as Buffett. They are the market and they cannot beat themselves. Their techniques may no longer work. Check out my success stories.
  http://tonyp4idea.blogspot.com/2015/09/successes.html

- The average performance of the hedge fund is terrible. You cannot depend on others to invest for you.

- One book describes ROE as the only theme (with the story of the life of the author to fill up the book). It is only one fundamental metric in my book. I modified P/E to include debt and cash for better predictability.

- **What to say** to your children why you did not buy him/her this book 30 years later. Colleges do not teach them how to achieve financial success but this book does. If you've achieved financial success after 30 years, do not thank me but thank the one who bought you this book.

My motivation to write this book

I would like to share my experiences, both good and bad. I use simple-to-follow techniques using the free (or low-cost) resources available to us. I have been successful in investing for decades. I am enjoying a comfortable financial life. I do not hold back my 'secrets' as my children are not interested in investing. It is my small legacy in sharing my investing ideas.

If you are looking how to make 100% return overnight, there are many other books claiming to do so and this book is not for you.

Market timing

The market timing works for the last two market plunges. It will work again in the next one as it depends on the falling stock prices. However, I hope it will give us the ample time to exit as the last two. This simple chart is the best-kept secret. I'm the one to publicize it and for doing that it makes a lot of folks angry with me. There is nothing to buy or subscribe as it is free from many websites.

It is better but not possible to sell at the top and buy at the bottom. I summarize these conditions in this book. After we've detected the market top conditions, use stops to protect our profits. I will describe a better way than stops to avoid flash crash.

The smart investor never sells at the peak as the peak is too risky.

Introduction

Most likely this book will not make you a billionaire. I'm not a billionaire. If I were one, do you think I have the time to write a book? It is used to catch your attention. The title "How to be a 10 millionaire" does not sound too appealing. When a child wants to be a president, most likely he or she will end up at least a good citizen. Aim high.

However, if you're young, 10 million (in 2020's money) is very doable. I separated this book into 4 stages on the road to become a "billionaire". If I had this book or a similar book when I started out, I could have made over 10 million by now. I hope my readers will.

When you are a recent college graduate, buy this book and start with Stage 1. It makes the ideal gift to a recent college graduate and s/he will thank you forever. It is truly a gift keeping on gifting. If you have the basic knowledge and time in investing, glance through Stage 1 and 2.

You do not learn from someone you do not respect. If some of my readers bought the 15 or so stocks mentioned in my article Amazing Returns, in a year they would have made more money than any other articles published in any investing site. Some asked me for proofs and some blamed me for high commission costs, etc. All these questions were due to no respect. The fact is it returned more than 50% in a year from the publish date and I claim to be the best performing article in a year for recommending more than 15 stocks in diversified sectors.

Stage 1

It is for young folks such as recent college graduates. Unless you are in investing industry, you do not want to spend a lot of time in investing. You have a life too! At this stage, concentrate in your career. Accumulate cash for an emergency fund to support you for six months and down payment for a house. Invest fully in Roth IRA (if you're eligible), at least the matched part of your 401K if available and ETFs for the extra fund.

Do not marry someone who spends money like no tomorrow. Contrary to the popular new belief, you should attend a good college even the monetary payback may not be good. You have a higher chance to find a compatible spouse with less chance of a divorce. A greasy lady graduated from a technical institute is not too appealing to me.

I design a simple plan on how to invest in ETFs and a simple way to time the market. It takes about 10 minutes on the first (or any) day of a month in investing.

Stage 2

Learn how to invest in the market. Use paper trade. I provide you all the tools. Depending on your time, learn stock investing but do not use real money. Knowledge means success. However, little and/or any misinterpretation could cost you money.

Stage 3

Invest in the market with real money. Start it small and increase your purchases gradually. It is the gut of this book covering most areas in profitable investing. The techniques are discussed in Advanced Topic Section. Stay away from day trading that this book does not describe; most newcomers lose money in day trading.

Stage 4

Protect your profits and donate some to the poor. In this stage, your health is more important than all the gold in the world.

Billionaires among us

Every generation has its opportunities to produce billionaires. In our generation, we have Bill Gates, Warren Buffett and many others. I prefer to set a 'modest' target of 10 million (in 2015's money) and be a turtle investor. Actually I know many folks with about a million dollars that are having a happy retirement. You do not need a billion to enjoy your retirement or have a happy life at least financially. Here is why:

Jesse Livermore, considered to be the greatest trader, made millions and bankrupted several times. Finally he committed suicide. It is better to be a turtle, boring investor. It is easy for the mind to make millions, but tough to lose millions. Examples abound.

I know two or three billionaires personally. They all have something in common: Participate in IPOs in Chinese companies. It is once-in-a-life-time opportunity to build bridges between the US and the Chinese businesses. It is similar to the Walton family making billions by importing Chinese products. What a simple idea and why did I miss it?

The objectives in life

We come to this earth with nothing and leave with nothing. Why do we fight for wealth, prestige and power? However, if we do not have the objective for wealth, prestige and power, it is a life without meaning at least for me.

Money should not be our primary objective in life and happiness and health have to be earned and cannot be bought with money. When you've accumulated enough wealth to have a comfortable financial life, you may want to pursue other objectives in life besides wealth.

I have seen many successful men and women who are not wealthy using financial yardsticks but they are wealthy in working in jobs they love, good friends, good families, good health and/or fulfilling their own objectives in life such as helping the poor.

Most likely when you've accumulated enough wealth for a financially secured life, there are many objectives in life more important than wealth such as happiness and health. Still not convinced? Check out the wealthy singers, movie stars and athletes. Are most of them really happy with all the broken marriages, drug and alcohol abuses…? I rest my case. Many of them do not have basic investing knowledge (most likely they have not read this book), and end up bankrupt.

I do not believe most authors on investing are rich. Unless they do it for fun, the successful ones do not want to reveal their secrets. As of this writing, I'm financially sound especially with my age and my frugal lifestyle. I do it for fun and I read my own books to remind me of my mistakes in investing. The best trader in our generation committed suicide losing all his money and called himself a loser. Learn from his failure: 1. He did not practice what he preached and 2. Risky bets. My books preach about being a turtle investor.

One friend accused me of my greedy investing. Does he favor the 1% or the 40% who do not pay any Federal income tax?

He accused the 1% (I do not belong in this group) of altering the tax laws to reduce their taxes. It is partly true and Buffett should not pay less than the tax rate of his secretary. Many rich folks donate their wealth to charities. Without the 60%, where do we have money to subsidize the 40%?

We should encourage the 40% to work. The current system takes away their benefits for taking a job. I contribute by paying income taxes when I make money in the stock market. A good market allows me to help the poor. Investors buy stocks to finance new products and services and hence boost employment. Capitalism is not evil.

The six pillars of success

They are hard work, persistence, innovation, honesty, passion and social responsibility, in random order. Why is luck not one of them? Most successful folks do not attribute the success to luck.

Also successful folks also are humble in learning how and why others are successful. Successful folks do make mistakes but they try hard not to repeat their mistakes. They also learn from others' mistakes. Now, you are ready to set your objectives and enjoy your road to wealth.

Why you want to gift this book
What should you tell your children about why you did not buy him/her this book 30 years from now? Colleges do not teach them how to achieve financial success but this book does. If you've achieved financial success after 30 years, do not thank me but thank the one who bought you this book – Pat your shoulder if you bought this book for yourself.

Important notices
© 2015-2022 Tony Pow. Email ID: pow_tony@yahoo.com

Version	Paperback	Kindle
1.0	05/15	05/15
2.0	02/20	02/20
3.0	02/21	02/21
3.1	03/22	03/22

No part of this book can be reproduced in any form without the written approval of the author.

Book store managers can order this book from Createspace.com. https://tonyp4idea.blogspot.com/2020/12/book-managers.html

Book update. https://ebmyth.blogspot.com/2020/12/updates-for-all-books.html

Disclaimer

Do not gamble with money that you cannot afford to lose. Past performance is a guideline and is not necessarily indicative of future results. All information is believed to be accurate, but there is not a guarantee. All the strategies including charts to detect market plunges described have no guarantee that they will make money and they may lose money. Do not trade without doing due diligence and be warned that most data may be obsolete. All my articles and the associated data are for informational and illustration purposes only. I'm not a professional investment counselor, a tax professional or any other field. Seek one before you make any investment decisions. Remember to consult with a registered financial adviser before making any investment decisions. The above mentioned also applies for all other advice such as on accounting, taxes, health and any topic mentioned in this book. Tax laws change all the time, so talk to your tax advisors before taking any action. Some articles may offend some one or some organization unintentionally. If I did, I'm sorry about that. I am politically and religiously neutral. I have provided my best efforts to ensure the accuracy of my articles. Data also from different sources was believed to be accurate. However, there is no guarantee that they are accurate and suitable for the current market conditions and /or your individual situations. The values of some parameters such as RSI(14) are arbitrarily set by me. My publisher and I are not liable for any damages in using this book or its contents.

How the rate of return is calculated

They are for education purposes only, and do not make your investing decisions based on them. I usually use annualized for better comparisons; 4% in a month is more than 5% in a year for example. For short-term strategies including momentum, shorting and year-end strategy, I use the returns for a month, and sometimes 2 months. For simplicity, most of my returns do not include commissions, exchange fees, order spread and dividends. The return = profit / investment. I am not and my publisher are not liable for any error.

How this book is organized

This book is divided into three sections: "Simple techniques", "How to be a billionaire" and "Advanced topics".

Even if you're experienced in investing, glance thru Section I, Simple Techniques.

This book uses many advanced strategies described in my other books but in the most simplified instructions. The trick is to incorporate advanced techniques and information from free sites such as Finviz.com and Fidelity.com.

The first strategy is simple market timing. You should not buy any stocks when the market is plunging. Actually you should sell most of the stocks you own when the market is plunging. I have a simple way to spot market plunges termed "Death Cross" ("Golden Cross" to return to the market). It is based on charts. However, you can obtain similar info without creating charts and there is nothing to subscribe to or buy. We have had more false signals recently; the indicator tells us to exit the market but return to the market shortly. In most cases, we do not lose much money except the tax consequences in taxable accounts.

The chart tells us when to reenter the market for the best opportunity to make money. I had about a return of 80% in my largest taxable account in 2009.

Section I: How to be a billionaire

Instructions on how to make a billion?

Most likely this book will not make you a billionaire. I'm not one myself. If I were one, do you think I have the time to write a book? It is used to catch your attention. The title "How to be a 10 millionaire" does not sound too appealing. When a child wants to be a president, most likely he will end up at least a good citizen. Aim high.

However, if you're young, 10 million (in 2020's money) is very doable. I separated this book into 4 stages. If I had this book or a similar book when I started out, I could have made over 10 million by now.

When you become a recent college graduate, buy this book and start with Stage 1. They do not teach you how to become rich in college. It makes the ideal gift for a recent college graduate and they will thank you forever. It is truly a gift that keeps on gifting.

There are more important objectives in life than seeking wealth such as happiness, health, relationship, etc. With wealth, a wise man can make the other objectives easier to obtain, but an unwise man can do the opposite. When you lose a lot of money and you're still smiling, you're a winner; the winner knows it is a temporary setback.

My friend died worrying about losing most of his life savings in the stock market. Eventually the market returned, but he was dead already.

Most of my friends making at least 2 million are investors in stocks, real estate or both. First we should be thankful as there are fewer wars than our parents and grandparents. It is easy to accumulate 2 million to retire in my generation.

Too conservative investors seldomly will be multi-millionaires unless you have inheritances and/or successful businesses. Our capitalistic system punishes us for not taking risks. You need to invest in stocks, real estate, or a combination of both. Both have advantages and disadvantages. The advantages of the former are usually disadvantages of the later, and vice versa. Most should invest in stocks and own his/her own house.

Advantages of investing stocks:

- Contrary to popular belief, investors are not parasites. You invest in companies that have good products / services, and punish poor management.
- Spend less effort unless you are a day trader. Invest in value companies and review them once a year and more often for swing investors.
- We can still invest when we are old, as investing does not need laborious energy.
- Do not have the problems in managing rental properties such as receiving rents and responses to repair/maintenance problems.
- The cost is low. Many brokers have zero commission cost. Be careful of the high-cost of borrowing from your broker.

Advantages of investing real estate:

- Tax advantages in the U.S (consult your tax advisor).
- High chance of long-term appreciation if the area is in a good location.
- Usually no need to swap properties.

From my observation, real estate investors are more frugal and mentally happier than stock investors; they do not know how much they gain or loss via the on-line statements. Small real estate investors need to be a handy man.

Stage 1

Unless you work in the investing industry, you do not want to spend a lot of time in investing. You have a life too I hope! At this stage, concentrate on your career. Accumulate cash for an emergency fund to support you for at least three months and a down payment for a house. Invest fully in a Roth IRA (if you're eligible), at least the matched part of your 401K if it is available to you and then ETFs for funds left over.

Do not marry someone who likes to spend money like there is no tomorrow. Contrary to the current popular belief, you should attend a good college even the monetary payback may not be good initially. You have a higher chance to find a compatible spouse.

I have designed a simple plan on how to invest in ETFs and a simple way to time the market. It takes about 10 minutes to invest on the first (or any specific) day of each month.

Stage 2

Learn how to invest in the market. Begin with using paper trades. I provide you with all the tools. Depending on your time, learn stock investing, but do not use real money initially. Knowledge leads to success. However, little and/or any misinterpretation could cost you money.

Stage 3

Invest in the market with real money. Start in small ways and increase your positions gradually. It is the gut of this book covering most areas in profitable investing. Stay away from the risky day trading; most newcomers lose money in day trading. Even many experts in day trading have their huge losses periodically. Value investing with market timing and trailing stops is the turtle way to make money in the long run. There is no substitution.

Stage 4

Protect your profits and donate some to the poor. There are more topics covered here. You should be very wealthy at this stage, if you have followed the book. Do not take extra risk on risky stocks. This is the time to enjoy your fruits in life.

Billionaires among us

Every generation has its opportunities to produce billionaires. In our generation, we have Bill Gates, Warren Buffett and many others. I prefer to set a 'modest' target of 10 million (in 2020's money). Actually I know many folks with about a million dollars enjoying a happy retirement. You do not need a billion to enjoy your retirement or have a happy life at least financially. Here is why:

Jesse Livermore, considered to be the greatest trader, made millions and bankrupted several times. Finally he committed suicide. It is better to be a turtle, boring investor. It is easy for the mind to make millions, but tough to lose millions. Examples abound.

I know four billionaires personally. The first two have something in common: Participated in IPOs in Chinese companies. It is once-in-a-life-time opportunity to build bridges between the US and the Chinese businesses. It is similar to Walton family making billions by importing Chinese products. What a simple idea and why I missed it? The other one is my high school classmate making movies in Hong Kong. Another classmate worked in MIT's post-graduate program and became one of the earliest employees of a famous drug company in the U.S.

The objectives in life

We come to this earth with nothing and leave with nothing. Why do we fight for wealth, prestige and power? However, if we do not have the objective for wealth, prestige and power, it is a life without meaning for most.

Money should not be our primary objective in life and happiness and health have to be earned and cannot be bought with money. When you've accumulated enough wealth to have a comfortable financial life, you may want to pursue other objectives in life besides wealth.

I have seen many successful men and women who are not wealthy using financial yardsticks but they are wealthy in working in jobs they love, good friends, good families, good health and/or fulfilling their own objectives in life such as helping the poor.

Check out the wealthy singers, movie stars and athletes. Are most of them really happy with all the broken marriages, drug and alcohol abuses? I rest my case. Many of them do not have basic investing knowledge (most likely they have not bought this $10 book and lose millions), and many end up bankrupted.

I do not believe most authors on investing are rich. Unless they do it for fun, the successful ones do not want to reveal their secrets. As of this writing, I'm financially sound especially with my age and my frugal lifestyle. I do it for fun and I read my own books to remind me of my mistakes in investing. The best trader in our generation committed suicide losing all his money and called himself a loser. Learn from his failure: 1. He did not practice what he preached and 2. Risky bets.

One of my friends accused the 1% (I do not belong in this group) of altering the tax laws to reduce their taxes. It is partly true and Buffett should not pay less than the tax rate of his secretary. However, many rich folks donate their wealth to charities.

Unfortunately only 60% in this country pay Federal income tax. We should encourage the other 40% to work. The current system takes away their benefits for taking a job. I contribute by paying income taxes when I make money in the stock market. A good market allows me to help the poor more. Investors buy stocks to finance new products and services and hence boost employment. Capitalism is not evil.

The six pillars of success

They are hard work, persistency, innovation, honesty, passion and social responsibility, in random order. Why luck is not one? Most successful folks do not attribute the success to luck.

Also successful folks also are humble in learning how and why others are successful. Successful folks do make mistakes, but they try hard not to repeat their mistakes. They also learn from others' mistakes. Now, you are ready to set your objectives and enjoy your road to wealth.

Until you retire, you should spend most of your time / effort in your career / business and NOT in the stock market. The swing in your portfolio would tempt you spending too much time in investing and that's not profitable in the long run.

Why you want to gift this book
What should you tell your children about why you did not buy him/her this book 30 years from now? Colleges do not teach them how to achieve financial success but this book does. If you've achieved financial success after 30 years, do not thank me but thank the one who bought you this book. Pat your shoulder if you bought this book for yourself.

The book "How to be a billionaire" is a perfect gift for college graduates. My other investing book for beginners is "Investing for Beginners".

1   Stage 1: Starting out

Why invest?

This is the only way to make money for the average person. Our capitalistic system punishes us for not taking risks (i.e. investing). It is easy to confirm when you compare the average returns of stocks and CDs in the last 30 years.

This stage requires you to spend minimum time by timing the market in its simplest form and buying ETFs that do not require a lot of knowledge and time to evaluate stocks.

Basic education / Simplest investing advice

Read basic investment articles for beginners. Both Fidelity and AAII (both require being a client or a subscriber) have excellent articles. Refer to "How to Start" in Section I. After you have funds for down payment of a house and emergency fund, I recommend buying ETFs such as SPY. When the market is plunging, sell the ETFs to accumulate cash. Move back to ETFs when the market recovers. For more aggressive investors, buy contra ETFs such as SH when the market is plunging.

Why market timing

Before 2000, market timing was a waste of time. However after that, we have had two market plunges with the average loss of about 45%. It sounds harder to time the market than it actually is. We have a simple technique to detect market plunges and when to reenter the market. Our objective is reducing the loss to 25%. Before you start Stage 2, practice what you have learned. Buy an ETF such as SPY that simulates the market when the market is not plunging.

Links
1 %: https://www.youtube.com/watch?v=ds5LQXBKtQg

2 Stage 2: Find & evaluate stocks

My steps to trade stocks

1. Search for valued stocks (from the proven screens).
2. Evaluate the screened stocks by:
    a. Fundamental Analysis.
    b. Intangible Analysis.
    c. Qualitative Analysis.
    d. Technical Analysis.
3. Sell stocks.

As with everything in life, there is no guarantee that this book will always make you money. However, the chance of success will be substantially improved especially when you practice all the ideas presented in this book. Start with paper trading first in this stage.

Screens (used to search stocks) are better than others in certain market conditions. You should have several screens and keep track of their recent performances. I prefer value stocks especially for beginners.

Learn about investing and test out some of the basic concepts. This stage gives you a foundation to the next stage that will use real money in trading stocks.

Continue market timing and trading ETFs as described in Stage 1. You're not ready to compete with professionals in trading stocks, but trading ETFs with market timing is fine.

Beside stock research

In this stage, you should enjoy the better things in life such as owning your own house and taking nice vacations. A trip to Washington DC should not cost a lot, but it is fun, memorable and a great learning experience especially if you have children. Buying a fancy car is consumption, and buying a decent house is an investment. Stick with investments.

3 Stage 3: Invest in stocks for profit

This is the gut of this book. I introduce long-term swing trading (i.e. keeping the stocks more than 6 months) as the first strategy.

In addition to Market Timing, Technical Analysis and Trade are included in this stage. You may want to start with mutual funds and/or ETFs. However, about one third of them cannot beat the market after fees. Depending on the time available, you may want to move a portion of your investments into portfolios managed by yourself.

4 Stage 4: Protect your wealth

Jesse Livermore, the best trader I believe, lost most of his fortune and committed suicide. Professor Irvin Fisher, the father of Wall Street, did not predict the 1929 crash and lost a bundle including most of his own life savings. Recently, the legendary Kirk Kerkorian's wealth reportedly reduced his portfolio from $16 billion in 2008 to $3.3 billion in March 2013. Examples abound.

This Stage introduces the following strategies: Sector Rotation, Insider Trading and Dividend investing. We should monitor our trades. Why are they big winners or big losers? Learn from both and trade accordingly. The rest is investment advice.

If you need a financial advisor, try to use the paid-for service. There is no free lunch and try not to buy their over-inflated services. When they try to sell you an annuity, run as fast as you can towards the exit door. Most annuities are written by the providers for their benefits. Very few have low-maintenance fees. However, the annuities before the market crash in 2020 perform better than the market. Do not attend any free seminars with fancy meals. Remember if you are the only one to buy their services, you have to pay for the meals for all the attendees.

5   For Retirees

The following describes my own experiences and yet everyone's situation is quite different. Check the current tax laws and consult your tax professional on any related topic. Also check my Disclaimer in the Introduction section.

Will and estate planning

They will lure you to their presentations by giving you meals at expensive restaurants. If your estate is small (such as below the Federal exemption), a simple will signed by a notary public and the assignments of beneficiaries in your broker's accounts may be sufficient. Gifting at the maximum limit allowed by law is a common and easy way to pass your estate to your children before you die.

Check the estate tax requirements in your state. Some investors move to another state that has more favorable estate tax treatment or even some people give up their US citizenship.

Many people transfer their houses to their children to avoid long-term care expenses. Check how to do it right with a professional.

I had several 'free' meals before I settled for my lawyer. He put my house into a joint trust. He advised me to put my largest taxable account into a trust account.

Taxes

I am lucky (or unlucky in considering how much taxes I pay) to have a higher tax rate in retirement than my working years due to my good investment return so far. Hence, it would be better for me not to postpone taxes during my work years. At 70 ½, we are required to withdraw our retirement accounts (except Roth IRA under the current tax law). Before 70½, I had converted some Roll-over IRA (used to be 401K during work) into Roth IRA as allowed under the tax law then. I paid taxes but it could be less at 70 ½ and/or if I start to annualize my annuity. Again everyone's tax situation is different and the tax laws may change.

Market Timing

Concentrate more on conservative investments such as CDs, Treasury bonds, safe corporate bonds and diversified ETFs. Save your emergency fund for at least three months after your retirement income.

From 1970-2000, the average annualized return is about 10%. Market timing may not help at all. However, since 2000, we had two market plunges (2000 and 2007) with an average loss of about 45%. For simplicity, read the chapter on "Simple market timing" and "Rotate four ETFs". For more detailed description, check out the chapter on Market Timing which shows you how to detect market plunges. To summarize:

- Do not invest during a market plunge.
- Invest aggressively in the early recovery phase of a market cycle.
- Invest conservatively during other phases with stop losses.

Make your money last

You may never run out of money if you withdraw 4% of your total asset every year.

http://moneyover55.about.com/od/RetirementAccountWithdrawals/a/What-Is-The-4-Rule-In-Retirement.htm

Health

I highly recommend the book China Study by Dr. Campbell. In short, eat more whole grains, vegetables and fruits particularly with different colors and avoid meats / dairy products. Replace milk with soy milk. Avoid cakes, cookies and potato chips. Exercise regularly. Maintain both good physical health and mental health. This is a start on health and I am no expert.

Enjoy your retirement life with hobbies and travelling as long as you are healthy.

More information

This book concentrates on investing and it tries not to duplicate the financial topics for retirees from many well-written books. I obtained the following books in Kindle format for 99 cents each from Amazon.com.

Retirement Financial Planning for Baby Boomers by Whitney Smith.

Retirement Solutions: Financial Strategies for Today's Retirees by Michael Dallas, CFP. More related articles:

Retire overseas. http://www.marketwatch.com/story/5-reasons-not-to-retire-in-the-us-2014-08-07

Managed Accounts. http://blogs.marketwatch.com/encore/2014/08/05/managed-accounts-too-pricey-for-retirees/

#Filler: War-like or war-addicted

We have 16 years of peace out of 242-year history. The price is too big to be the big brother and the global police. Some wars such as Vietnam and Afghanistan were just wrong wars for us. This is the U.N.'s job, not ours. We have so many problems to fix at home such as homeless, drug / alcohol addictions, disaster control, shooting...

6   Billion-dollar ideas

Being good in your profession normally leads you to a rewarding life. Being good at investing would make you financially wealthy and that is what this book is about. Starting a business would make you very wealthy or make you very poor. The pandemic of 2020 bankrupts a lot of businesses.

Three out of four new businesses fail in the first few years. Jobs, Gates and Zuckerberg are good examples of success stories. However, they are the exceptions. After watching the Million Dollar Idea from the History Channel, I conclude:

- You need to have an innovative idea to start and it has not been used before.
- Every generation has its own opportunities. The three mentioned have their opportunities in the new PC. The internet has made a lot of billionaires.
- The clip-on lens inventor from the TV show has the opportunity of add-on to the successful iPhones. Clipping on others' success is not a bad idea, but it may not last long for profits without future products.
- Very few starters can afford advertising. Market share does not mean profit. Many advertisers of internet products in the Super Bowl 2000 went bankrupt.
- Investing with minimal cost such as at a trade show gains publicity.
- TV shows and magazines will knock on your door if your product is innovative. It will help them to attract viewers. It is free and effective advertising.
- Need to protect your product by patenting and keeping secrets during early development. You cannot save money in this area.
- Most inventors are not good businessmen. You want to let professionals run your business, but you have to keep an eagle eye on it.
- Be prepared to make a budget during early development, and plan to secure extra financing when the budget is exceeded – it usually does.
- Prepare for hard work.
- If your spouse does not join you in your venture, you have to choose between fulfilling your dream and keeping your spouse.

That's why so many successful entrepreneurs are single while starting their ventures.

- Prepare for failure and how/when to exit.
- Most new products have to go through many milestones before they become marketable products.
- Ensure your product is not a fad after its initial success. Follow-up products should be planned.
- Face the reality.

To illustrate, do not allow your bias on China to cover your eyes on business decisions. Many businessmen such as Walton and Apple contribute part of their successes to China. For some products, assemble them in South China as they already have component manufacturer's close by, cheap labor, fewer regulations and a large internal market. After the pandemic of 2020, it may change.

My own experiences

You may be thinking I'm giving advice from others' experiences. I did run a one-man company named Micro Architect selling software for over five years. My opportunity was that there was little or no software for the first (arguable) personal computer, the Tandy computer. What was driving me to work hard was my dream to think big and my passion was to make good money.

I wrote about 10 software programs. I spent money on two ads and gained a lot of publicity via press releases. I attended PC computer shows once a year in Boston. My wife's insurance covered the entire family. Larger companies have a team of more than 10 programmers developing a program compared to one person writing 10 programs. My exit strategy was looking for a full-time job when I found out my new programs did not sell well. I used a blanket to watch TV in the cold wintry days more than 10 years before they invented the blanket with sleeves. My friend thought about the won-ton making machines long before any such machine was available. If we only dream without actions, we will have to bring our regrets and ideas to our graves. Even if we fail, we will have no regrets.

Filler:

In any business, we can learn a lot from Bill Belichick. It is the same for stock research, we need to have knowledge, leave no stone unturned, work hard... Luck has nothing to do with success for most successful folks.

7   Billionaires' errors

Many millionaires (with assets over 10 M) I know have made fatal mistakes. Many should take good care of their health, enjoy their family and protect their wealth or forget their objectives in life. That's why most big lottery winners are not happy.

- With the millions, some eat and drink carelessly. Some do not exercise enough. Many die early.
- Many always work more than 100%. At least one person I know died early during playing tennis, so know your limits.
- Many 'smart' investors end up bankrupt. One more zero added to your net worth does not mean anything to them, but losing all will.
- Many famous singers and athletes die early or end up bankrupt. Many are drug addicts and some pass their problems on to the next generation.
- When it is time to retire, enjoy life and do not start a new business.

How I retired earlier
I retired in my 50s. My wife's insurance covered us for life. I am spending most of the time learning and testing investing strategies. Here are my comments with others on this topic.

- Do not borrow money and/or max out your credit cards except for the primary residence.
- Have an emergency fund up to at least lasting for 3 months.
- You do not need fancy stuff to make you happy.
- Invest in a weighted ETF for large companies such as SPY and spend a few minutes in market timing as described in this book.
- Invest your time and knowledge in maintaining good wealth.
- Marry your spouse with the same objective in your financial life.

Filler 12 noon is not 12 pm
The Chinese restaurant I went to says they are open at 12 am. Are they wrong or is the world wrong? The next hour after 11 am is 12 am, NOT 12 pm.

ETF	Normal	Today (2/2021)	Crashing[5]
SPY[1]	40%	30%	0%
QQQ[2]	5%	10%	0%
ARKK[2]	5%	0%	0%
VTIAX[3]	20%	5%	0%
LQD[3]	15%	20%	5%
GLD	5%	15%	15%
CD	5%	0%	0%
Cash	5%	20%	60%[6]
SH[4]	0%	0%	5%
PSQ[4]	0%	0%	15%

[1] VOO is a low-fee alternative for SPY.

[2] QQQ has more tech stocks, while ARKK is an actively managed ETF specializing in 'disruptive technologies'. During market crashes, avoid them, esp. ARKK.

[3] VTIAX is an ETF for global companies. LQD is an ETF for corporate bonds.

[4] SH and PSQ are contra ETF to SPY and QQQ. They are shorting the corresponding index. When the market is recovering, switch them back to SPY and QQQ.

[5] Need to balance the allocations about two times a year as ETFs can grow or shrink. When the market crashes, rebalance it right away. All markets will crash, and the last two (2000 and 2008) have an average loss of about 45%. Refer to the chapter "Simplest marketing timing".

[6] Today's low interest rate does not benefit us for CDs. I would leave the cash not invested and wait for the recovery to move back to stocks.

Of course, everyone's situation is different. If you are conservative, do not buy SH and PSQ. If you are afraid of inflation (especially due to the excessive printing of money), allocate more on GLD, a gold ETF.

Do not listen to financial news. They are used by institutional investors / analysts to manipulate the market. Many times they act the opposite from what they preach. This is the primary reason retail investors do not do better. With the GameStop incident, do not invest in most hedge funds. Buffett has proved the hedge funds with their high fees cannot buy an indexed ETF such as SPY.

The above is my recommendation. In the long run, it should work fine. Consult your financial advisor before taking actions. Most info is from RainIsHere, a Cantonese YouTuber.

#Filler: Simple measures to reduce net security.
Do not click any links from unknown sources. Some seem to be ok but not.
MalwareBytes, for checking viruses, is free for download (they do not pay me).

Personally, I use a Chromebook for my financial transactions and a two-factor login for my stock trading.

#Filler "How to make a 50% return"

https://www.youtube.com/watch?v=eEto5nEkf1Y

#Filler Buffett, the person.
https://www.youtube.com/watch?v=w-eX4sZi-Zs

ETF	Normal	Today (2/2021)	Crashing[5]
SPY[1]	40%	30%	0%
QQQ[2]	5%	10%	0%
ARKK[2]	5%	0%	0%
VTIAX[3]	20%	5%	0%
LQD[3]	15%	20%	5%
GLD	5%	15%	15%
CD	5%	0%	0%
Cash	5%	20%	60%[6]
SH[4]	0%	0%	5%
PSQ[4]	0%	0%	15%

[1] VOO is a low-fee alternative for SPY.

[2] QQQ has more tech stocks, while ARKK is an actively managed ETF specializing in 'disruptive technologies'. During market crashes, avoid them, esp. ARKK.

[3] VTIAX is an ETF for global companies. LQD is an ETF for corporate bonds.

[4] SH and PSQ are contra ETF to SPY and QQQ. They are shorting the corresponding index. When the market is recovering, switch them back to SPY and QQQ.

[5] Need to balance the allocations about two times a year as ETFs can grow or shrink. When the market crashes, rebalance it right away. All markets will crash, and the last two (2000 and 2008) have an average loss of about 45%. Refer to the chapter "Simplest marketing timing".

[6] Today's low interest rate does not benefit us for CDs. I would leave the cash not invested and wait for the recovery to move back to stocks.

Of course, everyone's situation is different. If you are conservative, do not buy SH and PSQ. If you are afraid of inflation (especially due to the excessive printing of money), allocate more on GLD, a gold ETF.

Do not listen to financial news. They are used by institutional investors / analysts to manipulate the market. Many times they act the opposite from what they preach. This is the primary reason retail investors do not do better. With the GameStop incident, do not invest in most hedge funds. Buffett has proved the hedge funds with their high fees cannot buy an indexed ETF such as SPY.

The above is my recommendation. In the long run, it should work fine. Consult your financial advisor before taking actions. Most info is from RainIsHere, a Cantonese YouTuber.

#Filler: Simple measures to reduce net security.
Do not click any links from unknown sources. Some seem to be ok but not.
MalwareBytes, for checking viruses, is free for download (they do not pay me).

Personally, I use a Chromebook for my financial transactions and a two-factor login for my stock trading.

#Filler "How to make a 50% return"

https://www.youtube.com/watch?v=eEto5nEkf1Y

#Filler Buffett, the person.
https://www.youtube.com/watch?v=w-eX4sZi-Zs

Section II: Simple Techniques

For starters, just trade ETFs such as SPY (an ETF simulating the market), and you can skip the rest of the book. It only takes a few minutes every month. When the market is not plunging, buy or keep SPY (or any ETF that stimulates the market); otherwise sell it. Do the opposite when the market is recovering.

If you have less than $50,000 to invest, just buy ETFs. Improve your investing skills by reading investment articles from this book and your broker's website. For example, Fidelity has a lot of information for investors.

Subscription to AAII is recommended. When your portfolio grows more than $50,000, invest on a subscription such as Value Line, GuruFocus, Zacks or IBD (more for momentum traders). Initially, use the information for paper trading on value stocks, which is usually available from brokers.

For the long term, knowledge is most important in your investing life and experience comes next. Retail investors have a lot of advantages over fund managers. However, I advise you NOT to be a trader. Hence, you should ignore the 'fabulous' trade systems that claim to be very profitable. Statistically most amateur traders lose money as they cannot compete with experienced, disciplined traders.

How to start

I recommend trading ETFs first and when the market is not risky. The very basic terms such as ETF are not fully explained here; try Investopedia for terms you need to know. Otherwise, this book would be doubled in size and it would bore most readers. Investopedia, your broker's website (especially Fidelity) and AAII (requiring subscription) provide many excellent articles. Alternatively, buy a book for beginners. Here are some freebies:

Click here for Morningstar classroom.
http://morningstar.com/cover/classroom.html
Click here for Vanguard.
https://investor.vanguard.com/investing/investor-education
Click here for Investopedia's Tutorials.
http://www.investopedia.com/university/
Click here for Yahoo!
http://finance.yahoo.com/education/begin_investing
Click here for Fidelity basic in investing.
https://www.fidelity.com/investment-guidance/investing-basics

1   Simplest market timing

Why market timing

Before 2000, market timing was a waste of time. However, after that, we have had two market plunges with the average loss of about 45%. It sounds harder to time the market than it actually is. We have a simple technique to detect market plunges and when to reenter the market. Our objective is reducing the loss to 25%.

Market timing depends on charts; the following describes how to use chart information without creating charts. Most charts will not identify the peaks and bottoms of the market as they depend on data (i.e., the stock prices). However, it would reduce further losses. It is simpler than it sounds. Just follow the procedure below.

The first part of this technique detects potential market plunges, and the second part advises you when to start reentering the market. It applies to individual stocks too. It also works to detect the trend of a sector (entering an ETF for the specific sector instead of SPY) and a specific stock.

How to detect market plunges without charts (similar to <u>Death Cross</u>)
1. Bring up Finviz.com.
2. Enter SPY (or any ETF that simulates the market) or RSP for equally weighed SPY.
3. If SMA-200% is positive, it indicates that the market plunge has not been detected and you can skip the following steps.
4. The market is plunging if SMA-50% is more negative than SMA-200%. To illustrate this condition, SMA-200% is -2% and SMA-50% is -5%.
5. Conservative investors should sell most stocks starting with the riskiest ones first such as the ones with negative earnings, high P/Es and/or high Debt/Equity. Obtain this info from Finviz.com by entering the symbol of the stock you own.
6. Aggressive investors should sell all stocks. Extremely aggressive investors should sell all stocks, buy contra ETFs, and even short stocks. I do not recommend beginners to be aggressive.

As of 2/12/2022, the following are from Finviz.com.

ETF	SMA-200	SMA-50	SMA-20	Death Cross?
SPY	-0.8%	-4.2%	-1.7%	Yes (Step #4)
RSP	-0.5%	-1.9%	0.4%	Yes (Step #4)

Both ETFs indicate the market is a confirmed crash from my indications using a technique similar to Death Cross. However, they are quite close, and we should keep an eye on these numbers. In this case, SMA-

20 has not been used. If it is a false alarm, golden cross would indicate it and you should return to equity; it could be quite common in volatile markets. The futures indicate that on Monday (2/14/22) the market would plunge further.

Another test is using SMA-350: When the current price is below SMA-300, it is a crash. SMA-20 has to be more negative than SMA-50 and it has not been used here.

When to return to the market (similar to Golden Cross)

Use the above in a reversed sense to detect whether the market has been recovering. However, when the SMA-200% turns positive, I would start buying value stocks (low P/E but the 'E' has to be positive, and/or low Debt/Equity).

1. Bring up Finviz.com.
2. Enter SPY (or any ETF that simulates the market).
3. If SMA-200% is negative, the market is not recovering, and you can skip the following steps.
4. Sell all contra ETFs and close all shorts if you have any.
5. Market recovery is confirmed when SMA-50% is more positive than SMA-200%. To illustrate this condition, SMA-200% is 2% and SMA-50% is 5%. Commit a large percent of cash (or all cash for aggressive investors) to stocks. If you do not know what to buy, buy SPY or an ETF that simulates the market.

How often to check the market timing indicators?

Do the above once a month. When the SPY price is closer to SMA actions percentage, perform the above once a week. The charts and data for market timing described in this book are based on SMA-350 (Simple Moving Average) that is more preferable than this simple procedure, but it requires some simple charting.

Nothing is perfect

If the market timing is perfect, there would be no poor folks. The major 'defects' are:

- It does not detect the peak / bottom as it depends on past data. However, it would save you a lot during the crash.
- It is hard to determine whether it is a correction or a crash.
- From 2000 to 2010, there was only one false signal. The indicator tells you to exit and then tells you to reenter the market shortly. In most cases, you do not lose a lot. After 2010, we have more false signals.
- The market may not be rational or may be influenced due to specific conditions such as excessive printing of USD. If you do not mind charting, use SMA 350 (or 400) using SPY. Buy when the price is above SMA-350 (or SMA-400), and sell otherwise. SMA-400 reduces the number of false signals, but it is not nimble.

2   Quick analysis of ETFs

Evaluate an ETF

ETFs are a basket of stocks according to the market, a specific sector, country or a specific theme.

Yahoo!Finance used to give the P/E of an ETF. Try to get it from ETFdb.com. Enter the symbol of the ETF such as XLU, and then select Valuation. If it is below 15 and above zero, it could be a value ETF. Also, if the current price is lower than its NAV, it is sold at a discount (or premium vice versa). Compare its YTD Return to SPY's.

Alternatively, get similar info from http://www.multpl.com/. In addition, this website provides the following metrics: Shiller P/E, Price/Sales, and Price/Book.

From Finviz.com, enter the ETF symbol. If SMA-20%, SMA-50% and SMA-200% are all positive, most likely the ETF is in an uptrend. To illustrate, SMA-200 is Simple Moving Average for the last 200 trading sessions (no trading on weekends and specific holidays). The percent is how much the stock price of the ETF is above the SMA. If the percent is negative, it means the stock price is below the SMA.

If your average holding period of your stocks is about 50 days, SMA-50% is more appropriate to you.

If RSI(14) > 65, it is probably oversold; if it is < 30, it is probably under-sold (indicating value).

In addition, ensure the ETF's average volume is high (I suggest more than 10,000 shares), the market cap is more than 300 M, and it has low fees. Most popular ETFs have these characteristics. Beginners should avoid leveraged ETFs.

How to determine if the sector has been recovered

It is easier to profit by following the uptrend of an ETF using the above info. It is hard to detect when the bottom of an ETF has been reached. If SMA-20%, SMA-50% and SMA-200% are all positive, most likely the ETF is in an uptrend or it has recovered. It does not always happen as predicted, so use stops to protect your investment.

An example

First, determine whether the market is risky. Most beginners should not invest in a risky market. Advanced investors can bet against the market or a specific sector by buying contra ETFs or puts.

Next, you want to limit the number of sector ETFs by selecting those that are either in an uptrend or hitting bottom (bottom is hard to predict). Personally, I prefer sectors with long-term uptrends (indicated by articles found in many websites including cnnfn.com and Seeking Alpha.

For illustration purposes only for deteriorating market conditions, I would select the following ETFs: SPY (simulating the market based on large companies) and XLP (consumer staples). XLP should perform better than XLY (consumer discretionary) during a recession as those products are the necessities.

Technical indicators such as SMA-50 (Simple Moving Average for the last 50 sessions), SMA-200 and RSI(14) are obtained from Finviz.com and the rest are obtained from Yahoo!Finance.com. After you buy the ETF, use a stop loss to protect your investment. For example, biotech sector moved up for many months until it crashed in 2015. Change the stop loss value every month to protect your gains in this case.

As of 2/5/2016	SPY	XLP (staples)	XLY (discreet.)
Price	190	50	71
NAV	192	50	73
• Technical			
SMA-50	-4%	0%	-7%
SMA-200	-6%	2%	-7%
RSI(14)	44	50	36
Other	Double bottom at $186		
• Fundamental			
P/E	17	20	19
Yield	2.1%	2.5%	1.5%
YTD return	-5%	0.5%	-5%
Net asset	174 B	9 B	10 B

Explanation

- The figures may not be identical among websites due to the dates they are using.
- XLY has the best discount among the 3 ETFs as most investors believe a recession is coming.
- XLP has less down trend among the 3 ETFs as expected.
- XLY is more undersold among the three as expected.
- Double bottom is a technical pattern that indicates the stock would surge upward.
- SPY has a better value according to its P/E.
- XLY's dividend is the least among the three as they have more tech companies in the ETF. They have to plow back the profits to research and development.
- XLP has the best YTD return among the three.
- As long as the asset is above 500 M (200 M for specialized ETFs), it is fine and all three pass this mark.

There are many metrics such as Debt/Equity not readily available from most websites. Many sites list the top holdings of a specific ETF. Just average the metrics of the top ten or so of its stock holdings.

#Filler: Illogical logic

If we do not test for the pandemic, we would have zero increase in this pandemic. Some silly folks buy this argument. What happens to the once-great country?

Filler: The problems of the U.S.

1. Our political system. We waste time arguing between the two parties. There is no long-term planning, as the other party could claim the credit. Same as corporations' CEOs who care about their yearly bonuses.
2. The politicians have to satisfy their voters. Today give them free cash by jacking up the printing press. And ignore the long-term consequences.
3. We have to protect our workers, our environment... Hence, we cannot compete with many countries.
4. We have spent too much on the military and ignore our crumbling infrastructure.
5. Historically no country can rule the world forever.
6. We blame China, but ignore how hard-working Chinese are.

An example

This example evaluates RING, a gold miner, using ETFdb and Finviz that are free from the web. The data is from July, 6, 2020.

Bring up ETFdb and enter RING in the search. There is basic info that are important to me: Sector (gold miners), Asset Size (Large-Cap), Issuer (iShares), Inception (Jan. 31, 2012), Expense Ratio (0.39%) and Tax Form (1099).

They fit all my requirements. The expense ratio is higher than most ETFs that simulate an index such as SPY. I try to trade ETFs using Tax Form 1099 in my taxable accounts. The large cap created about 8 years ago by a reputable company is good.

Select "Dividend and Valuation". P/E of 17.39 is fine in a rank of 11 in 27 in a similar group of ETFs. As in my books, I stated it is hard to evaluate miners. I buy this ETF primarily to fight the possibility of inflation and the potential depreciation of USD. The dividend rate of 0.52% (0.70% from Finviz) is in the low range of the scale; it is fine for me as dividend is not my concern.

There is more info from this website. For simplicity, bring up Finviz:
- The short-term trend is up (SMA-20% = 8% and SMA-50% = 7%).
- The long-term trend is up (SMA-200% = 26%).
- It is close to overbought (RSI(14) = 64%; 65% to me is overbought).
- It is -4% from 52-w High. It has performed well from the YTD, Last Year, Last Quarter, Last Month and Last Week.
- It almost doubled in price from mid-March this year.
- Avg. Vol. is fine.

From ETFdb, check the Holding. It has 39 stocks, so it is quite diversified for this industry. The two top holdings are NEM (19%) and ABX (18%), which is listed as GOLD in NYSX. I also consider buying these two stocks in addition to RING. You can estimate the other metrics that are not available by averaging these two stocks. Here is my summary:

STOCK	NEM	GOLD
Forward P/E	20	25
Debt / Share	0.31	0.24
ROE	17%	22%
Sales Q/Q	43%	30%
EPS Q/Q	389%	254%
SMA50	2%	4%
RSI(14)	59%	60%
Insider Trans	-13%	N/A

Fidelity's Equity Summary Score	6.1	6.8

3 Rotate four ETFs

We can beat the market by rotating one ETF that represents the market such as SPY and cash via market timing. Aggressive investors can add SH or PSQ (contra ETFs) to the four to have better returns during market plunges.

During a market uptrend, rotating the following four ETFs could be more profitable than staying with SPY (or any ETF that simulates the market). Be warned that a short-term capital gain in taxable accounts is not treated as favorably as the long-term capital gain; check current tax laws.

The allocation percentages depend on your individual risk tolerance. You can use indexed mutual funds. Compare their expenses and restrictions. Some mutual funds charge you if you withdraw within a specific time period.

Select the best performer of last month (from Seeking Alpha, cnnFn, or one of many ETF/mutual fund sites). Add a contra ETF such as SH to take advantage of a falling market for more aggressive investors. Add sector ETFs to the described four ETFs such as XLY, XLP, XLE, XLF, XLU, IYW, XHB, IYM, OIL and XLU to expand your selection.

ETFs	Money Market	U.S.	International	Bond
Fidelity		Spartan Total Market	Spartan Global Market	Spartan US Bond
Vanguard		Total Stock Market	Total International Market	Total Bond Market
My choice	Fidelity	SPY	Vanguard	Fidelity
Suggest %				
During Market plunge	90%	0%	0%	10%
After plunge	10%	60%	20%	10%

Explanation

- The above are suggestions only. If your broker offers similar ETFs, consider using them.
- Check out any restrictions of the ETFs and commissions.
- 4 ETFs (one actually is a money market fund) are enough for most starters. They are diversified, low-cost and you do not need rebalancing except during a market plunge.
- The percentages are suggestions only. If you are less risk tolerant, allocate more to a money market fund, CD and/or bond ETF.
- Have at least 10% allocated to the money market fund for safety.
- When the market is risky, reduce stock equities (i.e., increase money market and bond allocations).
- The symbols for Fidelity ETFs are FSTMX, FSGDX and FBIDX.
- The symbols for Vanguard ETFs are VTSMX, VGTSX and VBMFX.
- If you are more advanced, use additional sector ETFs to rotate. Also buy long-term bond funds (such as 30-year Treasury) when the interest rate is 10% or more.

#Filler: Glad to be an investor

After watching the following YouTube video, I am glad my parents did not push me to play piano and also glad I do not have any musical gene. How can I compete with this kid?

https://www.youtube.com/watch?v=yf0B4rVoq44

Also, glad not into some life-threatening professions such as surgical doctors, soldiers, fire fighters, etc. I can make mistakes in investing from time to time without suffering from the consequences. With the uptrend market for most of the last 50 years, most investors should make good money. Thank God.

#Filler: Where common sense is not common sense

Excessive printing of money is not a long-term solution. Servicing the huge debt weakens our competitiveness. The politicians just want to buy votes today and finance their campaigns. Our next generations have to pay for these huge debts.

4   Simplest ways to evaluate stocks

Beginners should trade ETFs only. This chapter is for the readers who are ready or getting ready to trade stocks. In general, ETFs are diversified, less volatile than trading stocks. However, stocks offer higher profit but higher risk.

Many stock researches have already been done recently and some are available free of charge. I have no affiliation with Fidelity except I retired from it. You can open an account with them with no balance. Their Equity Summary Score is one of the best indicators; I check out **value** stocks with scores higher than 8. Concentrate on fundamental metrics such as P/E for long-term holds, and momentum metrics for short-term holds. Add criteria to limit the number of screened stocks. Finviz.com is a free screener.

Several sources

The popular ones are Morningstar, Value Line, The Street and Zacks (currently free for rankings of individual stocks). If they are not free, check out whether they are available from your local library. I have 3 simple ways to evaluate stocks starting with the simplest. In addition, read the articles on the selected stocks from Fidelity, Finviz, Seeking Alpha and many other sources for further evaluation.

Fidelity

Select only stocks that have Fidelity's Equity Summary Score 8 or higher. There are tons of information about a stock. Once in a while I did not agree with this score such as SHOP and ZM that scored high in August, 2020. Include the following for your analysis.

A modified stock selection based on a magazine article

Most metrics are available from Finviz except EV/EBITDA.

1. Forward P/E (expected earnings and not based on the last twelve months). It should range from 5 to 15 (10 to 25 for high tech stocks). EV/EBITDA (from Yahoo!Finance) is a better choice as it includes the debts and cash than P/E; it would be more effective if it uses forward earnings. If you do not use EV/EBITDA,

ensure Debt/Equity is less than 0.5 except for the debt-intensive industries.

2. ROE (Return of Equity) measures how well the company uses the capital. I prefer stocks with ROE greater than 5%.

3. Volatility. Conservative investors should select stocks with a beta of less than one (i.e., less volatile).

4. Insider Transactions for sales (i.e., negative) should be less than 5%. If it is -5%, most likely the insiders are dumping it.

5. Compare the metrics such as P/E and Debt/Equity to its five-year average and its competitors (available in Fidelity).

6. Momentum. Check out the SMA-50 (actually SMA-50%) and SMA-200. Ideally, they should be positive. SMA-50% is especially important for stocks you do not want to keep for a long time.

7. Check out articles on the stock as some recent events (for example a new lawsuit) have not been included in the metrics.

8. Compare the trend of the sector this stock is in. Under Finviz, enter the related sector ETF.

Summary
The sources are Fidelity (Equity Summary Score and various comparisons), Finviz and Yahoo!Finance (for EV/EBITDA). Value stocks should be held longer.

Category	Score / Metric	Value /Momentum
Score	Fidelity's Equity Summary Score	Both
Value	EV/EBITDA	Value
	P/E cheaper compared to 5-year avg.	Value
	P/E cheaper compared to its sector.	Value
	Insider Purchases	Both
Safety	Debt/Equity	Value

		Compare it to its sector.	Value
Momentum		50-SMA%	Momentum
		200-SMA% (for long term holds).	Value
Articles		Check out latest events	Both
Market		No purchase if market is risky.	Momentum

A simple scoring system using Finviz

Bring up Finviz.com and then enter the stock symbol.

No.	Metric	Good	Bad	Score
1	Forward P/E[1]	Between 2.5 and 12.5, Score = 2	> 50 or < 0, Score = -1	
2	P/ FCF[1]	< 12, Score = 1	>30 or < 0, Score = -1	
3	P/S[1]	< 0.8, Score = 1	< 0, Score = -1	
4	P/ B[1]	< 1, Score = 1	< 0, Score = -1	
	Compare quarter to quarter of last year			
5	Sales Q/Q	> 15%, Score = 1	< 0, Score = -1	
6	EPS Q/Q	> 20% , Score = 1	< 0, Score = -1	
			Grand Score	
	Stock Symbol Date[2]	Current Price	SPY	

Footnote

[1] Negative values for Sales (due to accounting adjustments), Equity and Book are possible but not likely.

[2] The last row is for your information only. SPY is used to measure whether it will beat the market by comparing the return of this stock to the return of SPY.

The Score

Score each metric and sum up all the scores giving the Grand Score. If the Grand Score is 3, the stock passes this scoring system. Even if it is a 2, it still deserves further analysis if you have time. You may want to add scores from other vendors. To illustrate on using

Fidelity, add 1 to the score if Fidelity's Equity Summary score is 8 or higher. Monitor the performance after every 6 months or so to see whether this scoring system beats the market.

Very basic advice for beginners

Beginners should stick with U.S. stocks with Market Cap greater than 800 M (million), Debt/Equity less than .25 (25%) except for debt-intensive industries such as utilities and airlines and Forward P/E between 5 to 20 (25 for high-tech companies). These metrics are all available from Finviz.com, which is free.

Do not have more than 20% of your portfolio in one stock (unless it is an ETF or mutual fund) and do not have more than 30% of your portfolio in one sector.

For more conservative investors, buy non-volatile stocks whose beta (available from Yahoo!Finance) is less than 1. Beta of 1 represents the market (the S&P 500 index). For example, a stock with beta 1.5 statistically fluctuates more than 50% of the market and hence it is very volatile.

Try paper trading to check out your strategy and your skill in trading stocks. If your broker does not provide one, use a spreadsheet to record your trades or check the availability of simulator.investopedia.com.

#Filler: Silence is golden

I am glad I did not give advice to a friend who had to decide whether to take a lump sum payment or an annuity. The correction in March, 2020 would wipe out a lot of his portfolio if he took the lump sum payment. No one would share his profits when the predictions are correct, but the blame if it does not materialize.

It is the same in investing that nothing is certain. With educated guesses, we should have more rights than wrongs especially in the long run.

5 Simplest technical analysis

When the stock, the sector that the stock is in and the market are all above its SMA-N averages (Single Moving Average for the last N sessions), most likely the stock is trending up.

1. Bring up Finviz.com from your browser.
2. Enter SPY. Write down the SMA-200 (Single Moving Average for 200 sessions). Positive numbers indicate that the trend for the market is up.

   However, the market could be peaking or overbought. Be careful when SMA-200 is over 5% and / or RSI(14) is over 65%. RSI is a metric on overbought / underbought.
3. Enter the sector ETF the stock is in. Write down the SMA-50. Positive numbers indicate that trend for the sector is up.

   However, the sector could be peaking or overbought. Be careful when the SMA-200 is over 10% and / or RSI(14) is over 65%.
4. Enter the stock symbol. If your average holding period of the stocks is 200, use SMA-200 and so on. I recommend SMA-200 for holding value stocks long term and SMA-50 for momentum stocks. Write down the SMA-N for your stock. Positive numbers indicate that the trend is up.

   However, the stock could be peaking or overbought. Be careful when the SMA-200 (or SMA-50) is over 25% and / or RSI(14) is over 65%.

If the above three criteria and the fundamental criteria are satisfied, most likely it is a good buy. If you buy sector ETFs or mutual funds only, you can skip step #4. In any case, use stop loss to protect your investment.

#Filler: The Ten Commandments of Investing.
http://www.investopedia.com/articles/basics/07/10commandments.asp

- Set goals. * Personal finances in order. * Ask questions. * Do not follow the herd. * Due diligence. * Be humble. * Be patient. * Be moderate. * No unnecessary churning. * Be safe. * Do not follow blindly.
- My additions: * Diversify. * Study market timing. * Protect your losses and profits. * Monitor your screens and your metrics. * Be emotionally detached from investments. * Learn from mistakes. * Stay away from bubbles. * Be socially responsible.

6   The best strategy

The best-kept secret in investing is to buy a weighed ETF. I use SPY as an example here. This ETF is well diversified as it keeps all 500 stocks in the S&P 500 index. The ETF has a higher position (in percentage) on stocks with higher market cap. The stocks with higher market caps usually grow the market cap by having good management and good products. The bad stocks are deleted from the index periodically.

The second best-kept secret is using simple market timing as described in this book to reduce the losses in market crashes.

It is very hard to beat this strategy. You do not need any knowledge in investing, and you only spend a few minutes every month to time the market. The market is risky when the metrics show you so such as the price is close to the simple moving average in using SMA-350 method; in this case you time the market more frequently.

7   Don'ts for beginners
- Do not use leverage: options, margin and leveraged ETFs.
- Do not short stocks.
- Buy low and sell high.
- Buy value stocks. Sell profitable stocks after a year and losers before holding 12 months for favorable tax treatments in non-retirement accounts. Be a turtle investor.
- Limit momentum trades.
- Use stops to protect your portfolio.
- Do not follow 'experts' blindly (most have their own agenda).
- Do not trade penny stocks (i.e., stocks less than 200 M and/or price less than $1 to my definitions).
- Venture into momentum trading when you have knowledge and time. Avoid trading systems that are available.
- Do not day trade. Most beginners lose most of their money.
- Do not take classes / seminars that promise you big money - if it works, they will give out their secrets.
- Be selective on investing subscriptions. If they give you a handful of stocks to thousands of subscribers, most likely the actual performance will not be good. Check their past performances that use real money.

8   Summary

The following improves the odds of success but there is no guarantee.

Risky Market?

Bring up Finviz.com. Enter SPY. If both SMA-50% and SMA-200% are both negative, do not invest especially when SMA-50% is more negative than SMA-200%.

Evaluate value stocks from others' researches

Gather a list of stocks from screens and/or recommendations from magazines. Use researches that are free. Value stocks should be kept for at least 6 months. In six months or so, evaluate the bought stocks again to see whether you want to sell the stocks. Some other sites may provide free trial or one-time evaluation: IBD, GuruFocus, Zacks and Morningstar. Fidelity requires an account but there is no minimum position.

Name	Pass Grade	Link
Fidelity's Equity Summary Score	>=8	
Value Line[2]	Timeliness > Average	
	Proj. 3-5 yr.% > 5%	
VectorVest[1]	VST > 1 and RV > 1	Link

1   Should be available from your local library.

2   Free for limited number of stocks and free trial.

Evaluate stocks

Bring up Finviz.com and enter the stock symbol.

Metric	Passing Grade
Forward P/E	Between 5 and 20 (25 for tech stocks)
P/FCF	< 15 and ratio is positive
Sales Q/Q	>10
EPS Q/Q	>15

Intangible Analysis

Bring up Finviz, Fidelity, Yahoo!Finance or Seeking Alpha (fewer articles now) and enter the stock symbol. To prevent manipulation, the stocks should have larger cap (> 200 M) and higher daily average volume (> 10,000 shares).

Bonus: Investing for 'lazy' folks

You have better things to do than investing or you do not have the time, the desire to learn and/or expertise in investing. You should be better off to buy ETFs.

I recommend the following 4 ETFs. If you have $100,000 to invest, buy $25,000 for each recommended ETF. Consult your financial advisor before taking any action. The recommended ETFs should have a large market cap (the ETFs themselves and not the stocks they hold) and have a high volume.

Most returns started on July 1 and ended on July 1 the following year; this article is written on July 20, 2021. All are annualized returns for easy comparison. Fees, commissions and dividends have not been included; you can add the dividend yield and prorate it for YTD return.

Symbol	Name	YTD[1] Return	1 Year[2]	5 Years[3]	Bear[4]
IWF	Russel 1000G	30%	34%	40%	-33%
QQQ	QQQ	30%	46%	42%	-31%
VTI	Vang. Viper Tot	34%	22%	42%	-35%
VUG	Vang. Growth	37%	33%	41%	-32%
Avg.		31%	34%	41%	-33%
SPY[5]		34%	21%	39%	-35%
Beat[6]		-9%	60%	6%	7%

[1] The start date is 1/4/2021 and the end date is 7/1/2021.
[2] The start date is 7/1/2020 and the end date is 7/1/2021.
[3] The start date is 7/1/2016 and the end date is 7/1/2021.
[4] The start date is 1/2/2008 and the end date is 4/1/2009. My estimates.
[5] SPY is the ETF for the S&P 500 index. It is used as a yardstick.
[6] = (Avg. − SPY) / SPY. Again, it does not include fees, commissions and dividends.

Comments:

- The YTD is the only period that this portfolio does not beat SPY (the market to many). It could mean the market could be changing the favorite from growth stocks to value stocks. However, 31% return is far above the average of the market.
- The one-year return beats the market by 60%.
- The 5-year return beats SPY only by 6%, but the return of 41% is nothing to sneeze at.
- All except Vanguard's Viper Total are ETFs for growth stocks. Hence, I expected it would not beat the market, but it still did by 7%.
- You can time the market using the techniques described in this book as often as you can. When the indicator tells you to exit, you can sell these ETFs and reenter the market when it recovers. Riskier investors can buy contra ETFs such as PSQ and SH instead of holding cash when the market is down.
- At least once in a year review the selection. Use ETFdb.com for information. If you do not have time, it is fine skipping the review. When you switch ETFs, taxes should be considered.
- Most ETFs replace some stocks periodically to ensure better appreciation potential.

Bonus: Sample portfolio

It is a suggested sample. You need to tailor it to fit your personal requirements and your risk tolerance. In general, you should have an emergency fund for at least 3 months (6 months preferred). Many of our generation have one or even no layoff. However, I estimate the current generation will have 3 layoffs in their work life. It is due to automation, artificial intelligence, global economy, etc.

The rough estimate of stock holding in distribution between stock and bond is equal to 100 – Your Age. To illustrate in the following three portfolios, I use a 30-year-old, and hence he should have 70% in stocks and 30% in bonds (including gold, CDs and cash).

In addition, some sectors are better than others according to the market conditions. The following three portfolios are for regular, todays' market and one during a market crash. I use low-cost ETFs exclusively. ETF is exchange-traded funds. They are traded similar to stocks, but most are more diversified; their fees are usually lower than mutual funds.

ETF	Normal	Today (2/2021)	Crashing[5]
SPY[1]	40%	30%	0%
QQQ[2]	5%	10%	0%
ARKK[2]	5%	0%	0%
VTIAX[3]	20%	5%	0%
LQD[3]	15%	20%	5%
GLD	5%	15%	15%
CD	5%	0%	0%
Cash	5%	20%	60%[6]
SH[4]	0%	0%	5%
PSQ[4]	0%	0%	15%

[1] VOO is a low-fee alternative for SPY.

[2] QQQ has more tech stocks, while ARKK is an actively managed ETF specializing in 'disruptive technologies'. During market crashes, avoid them, esp. ARKK.

[3] VTIAX is an ETF for global companies. LQD is an ETF for corporate bonds.

[4] SH and PSQ are contra ETF to SPY and QQQ. They are shorting the corresponding index. When the market is recovering, switch them back to SPY and QQQ.

[5] Need to balance the allocations about two times a year as ETFs can grow or shrink. When the market crashes, rebalance it right away. All markets will crash, and the last two (2000 and 2008) have an average loss of about 45%. Refer to the chapter "Simplest marketing timing".

[6] Today's low interest rate does not benefit us for CDs. I would leave the cash not invested and wait for the recovery to move back to stocks.

Of course, everyone's situation is different. If you are conservative, do not buy SH and PSQ. If you are afraid of inflation (especially due to the excessive printing of money), allocate more on GLD, a gold ETF.

Do not listen to financial news. They are used by institutional investors / analysts to manipulate the market. Many times they act the opposite from what they preach. This is the primary reason retail investors do not do better. With the GameStop incident, do not invest in most hedge funds. Buffett has proved the hedge funds with their high fees cannot buy an indexed ETF such as SPY.

The above is my recommendation. In the long run, it should work fine. Consult your financial advisor before taking actions. Most info is from RainIsHere, a Cantonese YouTuber.

#Filler: Simple measures to reduce net security.
Do not click any links from unknown sources. Some seem to be ok but not.
MalwareBytes, for checking viruses, is free for download (they do not pay me).

Personally, I use a Chromebook for my financial transactions and a two-factor login for my stock trading.

#Filler "How to make a 50% return"

https://www.youtube.com/watch?v=eEto5nEkf1Y

Section III: Advanced topics for each phase

Stage 1: Starting out

Basic education

Read basic investment articles for beginners. Both Fidelity and AAII (both require being a client or a member) have excellent articles. Alternatively, buy a book for beginners. To include all the basic terms and concepts, I have to double the size of this book which is already lengthy and bore most readers who already have the basic knowledge.

Click here for Morningstar classroom.
http://morningstar.com/cover/classroom.html
Click here for Vanguard.
https://investor.vanguard.com/investing/investor-education
Click here for Investopedia's Tutorials.
http://www.investopedia.com/university/
Click here for Yahoo!
http://finance.yahoo.com/education/begin_investing
Click here for Fidelity basic in investing.
https://www.fidelity.com/investment-guidance/investing-basics

Why market timing

Most do not understand why we need to time the market. Before 2000, market timing is a waste of time. However after that, we have two market plunges with the average loss of about 45%. It sounds harder to time the market than it actually is. We have a simple technique detect market plunges and when to reenter the market. Some ETFs are better than others.

1   The power of market timing

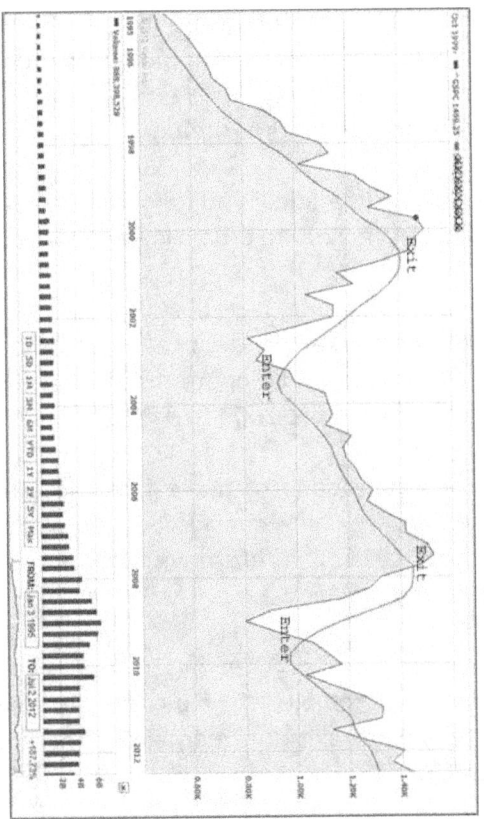

Detecting market plunges indicates the exit points and reentry points from 2000 to 9-2009 as follows.

Table: Vital Dates

Market Plunge	Peak	Bottom	Indicator Exit	Indicator Reenter
2000	08/28/00	09/20/02	10/01/00	06/01/03
2007	10/12/07	03/06/09	02/01/08	09/01/09
			08/01/11	11/01/11

As of 04/2014, my chart (from Yahoo!Finance) still indicates to invest fully in the market. For simplicity I skip a few brief exits and reentries since 2011. Run the simple chart once a month. When it indicates a potential market plunge is closer, run the chart once a week.

It is based on stock prices so it may not identify the peaks and bottoms precisely, but so far it has never failed to avoid big losses and ensure big gains by reentering the market. Hope it will give us enough time to act in the next market plunge as the last two did.

Unbelievable return with market timing

Calculate how much you made if you followed the above exit points and reenter points from 2000 to today. I bet you would make a good fortune.

To test the effect of market timing, I calculated the return of S&P 500 with market timing and compare it to the return of S&P 500 without market timing from 1-2000 to 9-2013.

There are many assumptions to make the calculations easier. In general, dividends are not considered. Compounding is not considered in most cases. The return with market timing should be substantially better if we buy a contra ETF during exits and sell it during reentries.

I was shocked by the incredible return by using simple market timing and the chart tells us to exit and reenter the market only 3 times from 2000 to 2013.
Summary info:

S&P 500 1-2000 to 9-2013	With Market Timing	Without Market Timing
Better	500%	
Gain	1,000	167
Gain %	68%	11%
Annualized gained	5%	1%
Days	4,959	4,959

Calculations:

S & P 500	With Market Timing	Without Market Timing
1-2000	$1,469^1$	$1,469^1$
Exit 10/01/00	$1,041^2$	1,041
Enter 06/01/03	1,041	964^4
Exit 02/01/08	$1,489^3$	$1,379^4$
Enter 09/01/09	1489	$1,020^5$
Exit 08/01/11	1,888	1,293
Enter 11/01/11	1,888	1,251
09/03/13	2,469	1.638
Gained	2,469 – 1,469=1,000	1,638-1,469=167
Gain %	1000/1469 = 68%	167/1469 = 11%
Annualized gained	68% * 365/4959=5%	11%*365/4959=1%
Better	(1,000-167)/167 = 500%	

Portfolio with Market Timing:

[1] Both start with S&P 500 of 1,469 on 1-3-2000.

[2] 10/01/00
The market timing portfolio exits the market and remains same value of 1,041 until 6/1/00.

[3]   02/01/08
The market timing portfolio exits the market and remains same value of 1,489 until 9/1/09.

'1,489' is calculated as follows:
1,041 * (1 + Rate) = 1,041 * (1 + 1,379-964)/964) = 1,489
where S&P 500 is 964 on 6/1/00 and 1,379 on 2/1/08.

The other calculations are based on S&P 500 is 1,020 on 9/1/9, 1,293 on 8/1/11, 1,251 on 11/1/11 and 1,636 on 9/3/13.

Portfolio without Market Timing:

[1] Both starts with S&P 500 of 1,469 on 1-3-2000. We could use the S&P 500 value on 9/3/13, but it will not account on some compounded interest consideration.

[4] &P 500 is 964 in 6/1/00 and 1,379 on 2/1/08.

[5] 02/01/08. The portfolio value is calculated to be 1,020 as follows:
   1,379 * (1 + Rate) = 1,379 * (1 + (1020-1379)/1379) = 1,020
   where S&P 500 is 1,379 on 2/1/08 and 1,020 on 9/1/09.

The other calculations are based on S&P 500 is 1,293 on 8/1/11, 1,251 on 11/1/11 and 1,636 on 9/3/13.

I cannot believe the shocking return with market timing. I checked my calculation and there was nothing wrong but do not hold me on this. Ignoring the compound rate of return should be minor. If you have time, send me your e-mail address to pow_tony@yahoo.com, so I can send you the spreadsheet to check out any error.

Even if I made a mistake somehow and got 100% instead of 500%, it still doubles the return without market timing! Ask any fund manager what it means to his or her fund performance and his / her career.

It will detect the next market plunges, but it may not give us ample of time to react as the last two did. It will not detect the precise bottoms and peaks as they depend on the stock price of an ETF representing the market. I have separate statistics on market peaks and bottoms but they have not been proven. The above may not work as effectively if there are too many followers. On the contrary it may work as it could be a self-fulfilling prophesy.

The stock prices of SPY are obtained from Yahoo!Finance. The entry and exit points are obtained from my simple chart from Yahoo!Finance described and they are subject to my interpretation.

Afterthoughts

- There are some noises (crossing the red line and backing again briefly) since 2011. The chart is not the only indicator I follow (that's why we have a book on this topic).

- Many including myself do not believe a market plunge is coming as of 1/2014. However, we have to be careful with the following analysis. Run the simple chart described in Chapter 6 to spot any indication of a market plunge at least once a month.

  - Among my top-performing screens for the last 3 months, many top-performed screens are from the peak stage (defined by me) than other stages in a market cycle.

  - The typical market cycle is about 4 years. We have about 6 years since 2007.

  - The stock market has not reached the bubble stage yet. It will if it continues to rise at this pace in 2013.

- On 6/20/2013, the market lost more than 2% in a day due to the Fed indicating no more easy money. The bond yield jumped. The Fed has been dumping about 1 trillion a year. When the money stops, the market would crash and the 2% loss seems to be a canary. Hopefully the current correction would be less than 10% [Update: only 6%]. Wall Street depends on the government handouts and the government is running out of tools to fix the economy. I expect the interest rates will rise gradually.

- Some REITs are inversely affected by the rising interest rate. http://seekingalpha.com/article/1570772-american-capital-mortgage-investment-was-the-baby-thrown-out-with-the-bathwater

- As of 1/2014, the market still keeps on climbing up despite our poor economy. I wrote:

  * About half of the total trades are driven by computers which can change their minds anytime and they could sell at the same time.

* The higher we climb, the steeper the cliff we will fall from.

Need to take action according to your individual risk tolerance. It is hard to convince the lottery winners not to buy lottery tickets. I had a hard time to tell my friends to exit in the beginning of 2000 when they made many times their regular incomes for 'working' 15 minutes a day.

- Will the market go even higher as of 1/2014? We have to compare the risk / reward ratio. If the risk is too high, we may want to take some chips off the table.

- I was accused of selling the secrets of detecting market plunges for less than $10. My reply:

  There are 4 groups of investors.
  1. Institutional investors. They vary in performances. In short, hedge funds as a group do not beat the market in the last 5 years.
  2. Mutual funds. Most cannot do market timing from their own regulations and as a group they do not beat the market after expenses.
  3. Most retail investors who are always on the wrong side of the market via fear and greed.
  4. While investors from #1 to #3 are losers, there must be some winners beating the market as a trade is a zero-sum game. In theory, we cannot beat the mutual fund managers who have better resources. However, we can use market timing to our advantage.

Links

- DRIP. http://www.fool.com/dripport/whataredrips.htm
- A similar NYT article was posted about the same time by the famous Professor Krugman.
http://www.nytimes.com/2013/05/10/opinion/krugman-bernanke-blower-of-bubbles.html?_r=2&

2 Market cycle

"Bull markets are born on pessimism, grow on skepticism, mature on optimism, and die on euphoria" - Sir John Templeton

The stock market has cycles as our practical interpretation of the above. It is about five years apart, but it fluctuates widely. I divide it into four stages: Bottom, Early Recovery, Up and Peak.

My defined four stages of a market cycle

We need to apply the right investing strategies to each of the four stages of the cycle.

- **Bottom**

   I would not invest for at least the first six months (or even a year) after the big plunge starts, which could lose over 25% in a few months. The exceptions are investing in contra ETFs and selling short for aggressive investors.

   I estimate it will take a year from the start of the plunge to the bottom, so I will normally sell stocks early in the plunge and do not buy stocks that are in the sector (sometimes sectors) that causes the bubble for about two years after the plunge.

   At the bottom, the high-yield corporate bonds (i.e. junk bonds) would prosper when the interest rates is decreasing to stimulate the economy.

   From mid-2007 to mid-2008, bonds suffered as the investors thought the sky was falling down - it was to those who lost the jobs and/or their houses. After that, some bonds especially the long-term bonds appreciated about 50% for the following year.

   The government lowered the interest rates and these bond prices with high interest rates surged. Correct timing in buying bonds could be very profitable.

   Long-term bonds have more impact by the interest rate: The lower the interest rate, the higher the bond prices of higher-yield bonds. The older bonds with higher interest rates are more valuable to the newer bonds with lower interest rates.

I define this period of the bottom from the start of the plunge to the start of Early Recovery.

- **Early Recovery**

It usually starts after one year from the plunge; no one can pin point the exact time consistently. By this time preferably earlier, we should have closed out all positions in contra ETFs and shorts.

Roughly speaking, October, 2007 (some use 2008) is the start of the market plunge. March, 2009 is the end of the bottom stage and the start of the early recovery stage of the 2007 cycle. However, every market cycle is different in where it starts and ends.

The one-year gain from the bottom is most profitable. It usually gains over 25% in a year from the market bottom. I, a conservative investor, had huge gains using some leverage in my largest taxable account in 2009. From my memory, I had a similar return in 2003 but I had not saved the statement as in 2009.

In this phase, value is a better parameter than growth in searching for stocks. If your investment subscription provides a composite value score and a composite timing score, the sort parameter of your screened stocks could be "Composite Value / Composite Timing" in descending order. Select the top stocks in this order. You still have to analyze the top-screened stocks.

Forward (same as Expected) P/E is a good metric. However, most companies may be losing money at this stage. Those companies that can last for more than one year with its cash reserve are potential good buys. The best appreciated stocks are beaten companies that have precious technologies and good customer bases. They could be candidates to be acquired if they are small enough.

- **Up**

  Usually the growth metrics such as PEG could be better than the value metrics such as expected P/E during this phase. Most stocks are winners except contra ETFs and shorting stocks. When the growth stocks are making headlines and the defensive stocks are being dumped, this is the hint that we're well into the Up phase of the market cycle.

  Locate stocks with growth metrics such as favorable PEG and high SMA-200% (from Finviz.com). Do not be scared on how much they have already appreciated. The strategy "Buy High and Sell Higher" works in this phase. Protect your profits with stops.

  Ensure that they have value too. Skip the stocks with expected P/Es higher than 35 unless there are good reasons. Most stocks will gain due to the tide of the market. However, when they're overbought (RSI(14) over 60), be careful. When institutional investors sell these stocks, they will crash.

- **Peak**

  When everyone makes easy money and the interest rates is high, watch out. Stop loss and/or stop limit should be used to protect your investment. Check out whether there is any bubble that would be burst like the internet in 2000 and the finance (and housing) in 2007.

  Internet crisis is easy to spot, but not the financial crisis. In 2007 we had a cycle longer than the average which is about 5 years. The plunge is very fast and very steep — thanks to the institutional investors who drive the market down.

  Run the technical analysis chart described in the Chapter on Spotting Big Market Plunges at least monthly (weekly if you have time). Protect your investment. Do not fall in love with any stock (you can buy it back later at a deep discount). Making the last buck is a fool's game.

  Accumulate cash according to your risk tolerance. A retiree or a conservative investor would accumulate from 25% to 50% and should be ready to move to all cash when the plunge starts.

We can lower the cash percent if we use enough stop loss protection. Be psychologically prepared because the stock market may still rise for a while. There is no perfect market timing.

The 2007 Cycle

The market plunged starting in 10-2007 and ending in 3-2009 (bottom), started to recover in 3-2009 (early recover), and trended up from 2010 to 1-2013 (the up phase of the market cycle). As of 3/2016, it is the peak phase defined by me.

As of 1/2013, we have recovered all the market losses since 2007. However, as of 7/2014, the economy has not fully recovered compared to the economy before the plunge. The employment judging by the medium salary has not fully recovered and the economy is not expanding. It is uncommon that the economy does not follow the market. It is due to the excessive supply of money by the government and partly due to globalization to allow companies to hire overseas.

Although a W-shaped recession seldom happens, we have a chance today. We hope we do not have a depression and/or the similar lost decades that Japan has been experiencing. Some may conclude we are close to completing a market cycle from 2007 to 2016. As of 2016, the economy is recovering slowly and we're better than most other global economies.

Again, market timing is not an exact science as it involves irrational human beings and government interventions. The timing using market cycle described here is a guideline as it is hard to time it exactly.

The average market cycle is about 5 years, but they fluctuate. If we consider 2007 as the plunge, we have about 8 years of this cycle as of 2015.

In a typical cycle (few are typical), we have about one year in each of the 4 phases I defined (plunge, early recovery, up and peak).

Events/Triggers

There are financial events and triggers that cause the transition of one phase of the market cycle to another. They usually do not change the sequence of the phases (say not from Peak to Early Recovery), but they may change the duration of the phase. Examples are:

- The government announcing change of the interest rate,
- Change of employment, and
- Change of GNP.

Sectors in a market cycle (my suggestion)

Market Phase	Favorable	Unfavorable
Early Recovery	Financial, Technology, Industrial	Energy, Telecom, Utilities
Up	Technology, Industrial, Housing	
Peak	Mineral, Health Care, Energy, Long-Term Bond, Consumer Discretionary	
Bottom	Consumer Staples, Utilities	Consumer Discretionary, Technology, Industrial, Long-Term & high-yield Bond

The sectors that cause the recession usually take a longer time to recover. In 2000, the technology sector was not favorable in the Early Recovery phase, contrary to the above table. In 2007, the financial sector was not favorable in the Early Recovery phase. These are the "offending" sectors that cause the plunges.

In a recession, we usually cannot cut down on consumer staples and utilities, but we can cut down on buying consumer gadgets. Companies usually postpone investing in equipment and systems during a recession and expand when the economy is humming. The government usually lowers the interest rates right after the plunge to stimulate the economy.

Conclusion

When the market is about to plunge or change from one stage to another, run the described chart more frequently and read more articles written by the experts.

Again, market timing is not an exact science but it is based on educated guesses. The better guesses should have more rights than wrongs in the long term. Our actions depend on our risk tolerance. Be careful on using any new strategy that has not been fully understood and proven. Since 2000, market timing is very important to your financial health with two market plunges with an average of about 45% loss.

3   *Spotting big market plunges*

This chapter is lengthy, complicated in some concepts and requiring you to try it yourself. Make your market decision by combining all the hints described in this article.

No one can consistently predict the correct stages of the market cycle. This chapter is intended for educational purpose only. However, if we have more rights than wrongs with our calculated and educated guesses, we should do well. As in everything in life, there is no guarantee.

There are my 11 hints to identify a market plunge. The average loss of market plunges from top to bottom for the last two crashes is about 45%. It could wipe out most gains for the entire market cycle. We target to avoid half of the loss.

Do not buy stocks during market plunge that could last for more than a year, which is defined by me from the market peak to the market bottom. It is a million-dollar decision for many including myself. This low-cost book serves as a reference and past performances do not guarantee future performances.

From 2000 to 2008, we only have one false signal for our SMA-350 out of 3 signals. Since then, we have more false signals. To adjust to this volatility, do not move everything to cash on an exit signal.

Adjust the amount of cash according to your own risk tolerance. Usually we do not lose much (sometimes we gain some) as another signal tells us to return to the market shortly. They only have tax consequences in taxable accounts.

Eleven hints of a market plunge

1. Technical analysis (TA).

    The following chart is created by Yahoo!Finance. If it does not display well on a small screen, copy the following link to your browser to display it on your PC.
    http://ebmyth.blogspot.com/2013/05/ta-graph-for-spotting-plunges-chapter.html

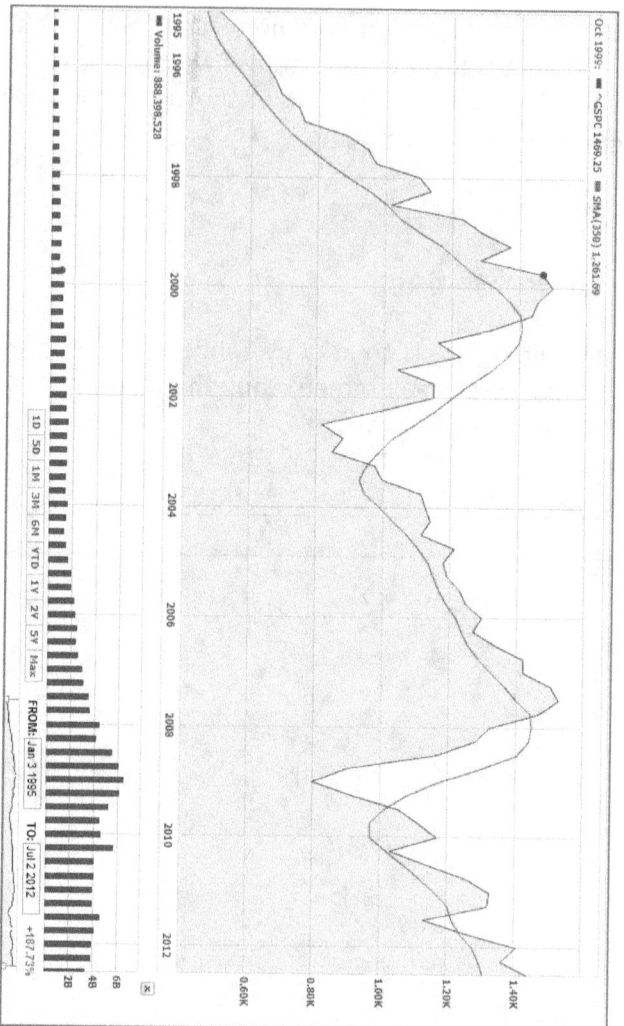

350 days simple moving average (SMA). Yahoo!Finance

The red line is the 350-day SMA, Simple Moving Average. If the stock price is below the moving average, it has detected a market plunge by this chart. Return to the market when the price is above the moving average line described as Early Recovery later. "350 days" are trading sessions. I have tried different "days" and 350 is the best fit for the last two market plunges, but it does not mean it would be the best fit the next market plunge.

We have two cycles described in the chart. From the above, we should leave the market in the first quarter of 2000 and return to the market on the first quarter of 2003.

On the second cycle, the chart tells us to get out in Dec. 2008 and come back in July 2009 approximately. Enlarge the chart by selecting 5 years instead of the maximum or use a larger monitor for a more detailed chart. The chart sometimes gives false signals to tell us to exit but tell us to reenter briefly. In most cases, we do not lose much except the tax consequences for selling. No technical indicators are perfect.

I started to come back on Feb. 2009. It was perfect timing but most likely or partly it was due to good luck. I was partially influenced by several articles I read.

Technical Analysis is based on the past data, so you cannot avoid the initial losses but it could reduce further and larger losses. From the above, the chart detected the two big plunges nicely allowing enough time to take actions. Will the next plunge be detected? It will I guess. However, it may not allow enough time as the last two.

Sometimes, we time it wrongly or prematurely and miss some gains by leaving the market too early. We need to treat it as buying insurance; it only pays big when the worst happens. When the "reward / risk" is too low, it is better to stay in cash. One's opinion.

Return to equity when the price is above the moving average (the red line). You should profit more by following the chart than 'Buy and Hold' or keeping your money under the pillow. For the last two market cycles, I returned to equities in Early Recovery (a stage of the market cycle defined by me) and profited. Can I be 100% sure for the next market plunge and come back in a timely order? Certainly not.

If most of your stocks are in tech, use QQQ instead of SPY. In addition QQQ is more volatile than SPY and the tech sector usually leads the market.

It can be created by following the steps; you need to create one yourself to detect the next plunge with current data.
- From Yahoo!Finance or any chart systems, enter SPY (or the S&P 500 index) or an ETF that represents the total market.
- Select Interactive Chart.
- Click Technical Indicators.
- Select SMA (simple moving average).

- Enter 350 days (actually it is trade sessions). Many chart systems use 'month' as unit, enter 12 or 11.67 if decimals is allowed (=350/12) instead of 350.
- Enter 1-3-2000 on "FROM:" or any "from date" that fits your screen.
- Select Draw.

Note. I switch to Fidelity for charting now as I cannot produce the same info from Yahoo!Finance. It could be my fault or a bug that should be fixed. If you cannot use Fidelity, try StockCharts.com.

2. Do the opposite of the flow of the dumb money.
When everyone is buying recklessly, making money and proclaiming that they are geniuses, sell. In 1999, my friend told me that he should quit his job and concentrate on investing as he was making many times in the stock market over his regular salary by spending half an hour a day. I would call myself a genius by making $1,000 an hour. When AAII's bullish sentiment (a contrary indicator to me) is over 70%, watch out.

On the same year, there were so many successful IPOs with '.com' names and these companies did not know how to make profits but blindly captured their market shares at all expenses.

They gave me $20 for just registering in their site. The poor quality of their ads showing their products during the Super Bowl reflected the quality of their management. The so-called 'MBA's business model' of capturing a potential market of one million potential sales by spending five millions is not Business 101 but Fool 101.

The inverse flow of money market funds is a good indicator too. The more money flowing into the equity funds by retail investors, the riskier is the market. Greed is a human nature. It is hard to resist buying stocks when your friends are all making good money in the market and you feel you do not want to miss the boat. I tried unsuccessfully to convince lottery winners not buying lottery and they showed me they had made another thousands yesterday.

3. Duration.
Cycles usually occur every four or five years. This is a very rough estimate as cycles often vary from 1 to 8 or even more years. After

the market plunge on 2007-2008, we are having (as of 12/2018) one of the longest bull market. The longer it stays at the peak, the higher the chance the market will plunge and the further it will sink. I call it Newton's Law of Gravity or 'What goes up must come down'. When we follow the charts (technical indicators), we still stay in the market most of the time.

4. Valuation.

The average historical P/E of S&P 500 is about 15 (or 16.5 depending on when you start the data). When it is over the average, be careful. Obtain the P/E of SPY (an ETF for S&P 500) from Yahoo!Finance and confirm it in many other sources. When the average P/E of a sector is over 35, most likely there will be a fierce correction for that sector. When it is over 40, the market most likely has peaked. When you find fewer value stocks than before, it means the market is riskier now.

The P/E of S&P 500 was 28 in 2000. It was 18 in 2007 and 16 in 2015. Both are over 15, the average value for the last five years.

The value of the average P/E has to be adjusted as the market conditions are not the same 10 or so years ago. Today (2016) part of the earning (the E in P/E) is due to the low cost in borrowing and less wage cost due to hiring overseas. Most global corporations can offshore jobs to reduce expenses. The global economies are inter-connected far better than before. When the global economies fall, we will fall too.

5. Triggers to burst a bubble.
In 2000, the trigger was the tech bubble. In 2007 it was the housing (or financing) bubble. It was easy to spot a massive tech bubble in 2000. I moved most of my tech sector funds to traditional sectors (cash for 20-20 hindsight) in the beginning of April, 2000, which was too close for comfort to this market plunge.

Most investors including myself did not understand the workings of the derivatives of the mortgage loans and could not recognize the bubble. I made good money in the oil sector in 2007. However, in 2008 most of my investments were losers including the investment in the oil sector. If I followed the hints described in this chapter, I would have avoided heavy losses.

6.   Rising interest rates.

It is more expensive for investors using margin to buy stocks, for companies to borrow money and for consumers to buy high ticket items and houses.

A related hint is rising margin debt (the debt used to buy stocks backed up by the current stock holdings). When we have a record margin debt as in 2016, the chance of a market plunge is high when the Fed hikes the interest rates.

When the Fed discount rate is 5% or above, be careful. This is also the time to buy long-term bonds. When it is 1% or less, most likely the market starts to recover. This is also the time NOT to buy long-term bonds. This strategy was proven in market cycles in 2000 and 2008.

7.   Yield Curve.

When the short-term (say 3 month) interest rates is higher than the long term (say 30 years), it is abnormal and a bearish signal. Click here to check the yield curve.

Many use two-year Treasury and ten-year Treasury. As of Oct. 15, 2018, they were 2.82% and 3.09% and it was very close to be equal and gave us some warning on a potential recession. You may want to move some of your risky investments such as stocks to safer investments such as CDs and short-term bonds. As of 2018, only two false warnings from the last seven recessions when an inverted yields occurred. Again, your action depends on your risk tolerance.

http://www.treasury.gov/resource-center/data-chart-center/interest-rates/Pages/TextView.aspx?data=yield
http://blogs.marketwatch.com/thetell/2014/05/13/bear-market-wont-come-until-the-yield-curve-says-so-kleintop/

8.   Rising oil price.
It is the same as the above as rising oil price will cause everything more expensive. However, today (2015-2016) is an exception. The falling oil price correlates with the market. It is due to falling too

much and the oil-producing countries have to dump the stocks to rescue their economies. If I have to put a number, I would say the market is risky when the oil price is below $30 or above $120.

9. Market experts.

There are always two camps predicting the market trend. Check out those that make sense and ignore those who try to sell you books or their services. The media try to scare you to improve the circulation. The reason I exited the market in April, 2000 is the result of reading an article that said the entire company of an internet company could fit into a conference room of a company with the same market cap. Good seeds fall in fertile soil will prosper. The opposite is true when bad seeds fall in any kind of soil.

10. Politics.

The long market rise from 2009 to 2016 is due to the low interest rates even the economy is not doing well. The interest rates is controlled by the Federal Reserve Bank, which is an agent of the government. After WW2, the market has never been down in a year right before election. As of 2016, the low-interest saves the market at the expense of our national debt which is at the recent peak. Trump's proposed 45% tariff could bring global recession starting in the US and China.

11. Miscellaneous.

In 2000, I exited the market after reading an article describing how the entire corporation fitting into a big conference of a large corporation. In 2008, we had a "Double Top" technical indicator that correctly told us a market plunge.

Be conservative

As in any new strategy, test it out and try it out gradually with real money. Most of you paid less than $25 for this book and most likely you do not want to risk all your money based on a $25 advice, so consult your financial advisors. You should not lose money by exiting the market too early, but miss the opportunity to make more money. If the market does not crash, treat it as insurance. No one can predict market directions consistently and correctly. This article gives you better hints to time the market and all markets are different.

The chart worked fine for the last two crashes, but as in life there is no guarantee to detect the next market crash for the following reasons:

- It may not give us ample of time to react as the last two. The current market is high and is caused by excessive money supply. When the money supply is reduced (or no more QEn), the market will react negatively.
- When too many folks buy my books and use the same chart, it will lose its effectiveness. It is most likely not, but there is always a chance.
- Past performances do not guarantee future performance.
- The market is not always rational.
- There are more noises (crossing the red line and backing again briefly) since 2011. The chart is not the only indicator I follow. Adjust it according to your risk tolerance.

Since 2011, there are several exits/entries as the market is not rational. However, if you follow it, you're still faring well as they tell you reentry very quickly. You do not lose or gain a lot by doing so. Even if you lose a little, it could be the best insurance you bought.

The noises would be increased if we use 200 days in SMA in the chart instead of 350. For the same reason, they will be decreased if I use 400 days but the signal will be later delayed.

As in life, there is nothing guaranteed, the chart is far better than market timing without charts and/or no market timing at all since 2000. As of 6/2015, I started looking at my charts more frequently months as we've been living dangerously on borrowed time for a long while.

4   Market timing by calendar

The following predictions are based on historical data. You may have slightly different findings depending on when you start and when you end your testing.

You can load the historical data of SPY via Yahoo!Finance and check out how close you are or different from my own predictions. They are my predictions based on historical data. Use it as a reference only.

- Presidential cycle.
  Usually the market performs worse in the first two years after the election than the next two. During the 3rd year the president has to make the economy look rosy in order to buy votes. Statistically it is the best year for the market and is followed by a good year (the election year). The government may stimulate the economy, the stock market and employment by printing more money, lowering interest rates and lowering taxes. The market in the 100 days before the election should be positive and less volatile according to 40 years of data.

  Democratic presidents have better market performance statistically than Republican presidents. This is not too logical as though Republicans are more pro-business traditionally.

- Olympics.
  It has been proven that the host country has a better chance that its stock market appreciates the year after the Olympics. It could be due to the exposure from the Olympics and / or the huge expenses in preparing for the Olympics.

  The last two Olympics follow this pattern as of 12/23/2013:

Olympics Country / Year	ETF	Period	Return
United Kingdom / 2012	EWU	Jan. 3, 2013 - Dec. 23,2013	11%
China / 2008	FXI	Jan. 3, 2009 - Dec. 31, 2009	43%

Greece could be an exception. It is too small a country to host this world-class event and it has wasted too many resources by building too many white elephants that the country can never justify. Brazil depends on its export of natural resources to China, so I do not count on the Olympics effect there.

Winning a lot of Olympic medals has no prediction for the stock markets. Both the Russian Empire and E. Germany were winners but disappeared in their original forms afterwards.

- Seasonal.
  Best profitable investment period is: Nov. 1 to April 30 of the following year. It is similar to the saying 'Sell in May and Go away'. It did not work since 2009 as it was an Early Recovery (defined by me) in the market cycle.

  The market does not always happen as predicted. However, when more folks follow this, it becomes a self-fulfilling prophecy. I prefer "Sell on April 15 and come back on Oct. 15" to act before the herd. The more practical strategy is to start selling in April 1 and become more aggressive (selling at closer to the market prices) when it is close to May 1. For the last five years, I did not find this prediction reliable.

  The explanation of the 'summer doldrums' could be that the investors cash their stocks for vacations and college tuition in the fall. Buying quality companies at the dips could be profitable.

- The worst month: September.
  The next worst month is October. However, if there is no serious market crash during October (and this month has more than its shares of crashes), it could be the best month to buy stocks.

- The best month for the bull: November.
  However, several market bottoms occurred in October and November. The next strong month is December.

- Best 30 days: Dec. 15 to Jan. 15, next year.
  It was correct for the period of 2012-2013.

- Window dressing.
  Institutional investors sell their losers and buy winners around Nov. 1. From my rough estimate and on the average, the winners have a 2% percentage point gain better than the market and the losers have 1% worse than the market.

I recommend that you evaluate the top 10 winners from the last 10 months or YTD in Oct. 15 and sell them at 3% gain or two months later.

I recommend that you buy in Dec. and sell them 3 months later. Include the stocks with more than 30% loss for the last 11 months or YTD, sort them by Earning Yield in descending order and evaluate the top 10 stocks.

In both cases, do not buy foreign stocks and stocks with return of capital. Ignore stocks not in the three major exchanges, with low volumes and stock prices less than $2. Do not buy in losing years such as 2007 and 2008. I have my tests with my own assumptions and I use tools not available to most readers.

This is a guideline only. Do not buy any stocks during market plunges. Current events should be considered first such as a potential war and the hiking of interest rates.

Afterthoughts

- I predict it will be a sideways market in the later part of 2013. I am following the sideways strategy: Buy on dips and sell when the market is ups. One's prediction.

- Why September has a bad reputation?
  http://www.marketwatch.com/story/betting-on-septembers-terrible-odds-2013-08-27?dist=beforebell

The September of 2013 (2 days away at the time of this writing) will have more problems. Check it out how many of the following are correct on Oc. 1, 2013. Use it as a future guideline to predict the next September using the current market conditions then:

1. The market is not excessively expensive, but it is not cheap. It is due for a 5% correction.
2. Unrest in Syria (check any unrest in your next prediction on September).
3. High oil prices due to Syria.

4. September is statistically a bad month for the stock market. However, it could be an opportunity to invest after the correction if any.
5. Interest rates is rising.
6. All the above indicate the market will dip. However, the rosier outlook is that the global economies are improving even slowly.

- January effect.
  The performance of January may determine how the entire year performs. I cannot find any rationale but it has been proven right statistically.

- Earnings period announced in Jan., April, July and Oct. would cause big swings in stocks when they have surprises. Earning revisions could be a good predictor.
  http://www.investopedia.com/terms/e/earningsseason.asp

Links
Presidential Cycle:
http://www.investopedia.com/articles/financial-theory/08/presidential-election-cycle.asp

Calendar-based market timing:
http://stock-chartist.com/2010/10/calendar-based-market-timing/

Calendar market timing for 2013:
http://www.investorecho.com/archives/8047

Filler: Golden Gate

Just minutes ago, my mail system asked me to sign in. I did and repeatedly they asked me to sign in again and again. I closed down everything and followed Gates' golden rule: If everything does not work, just power down everything and power it up again. I did this and prayed too. It works. Thanks Gates for fixing my problem.

There is NO one doing BASIC quality control. If it happened in my generation, many guys would be fired. Mediocrity is the new norm?

5   Market timing example

The market is making new highs. There are always two camps of market timers. One camp predicts a crash is coming while the other predicts it will continue making new highs. This article includes both arguments and suggests how and what actions you need to take to protect your investments.

Management summary

The market is fundamentally unsound evidenced by fundamental metrics but technically sound evidenced by technical metrics that both will be described in this article. The data were obtained on 09/22/2018. The market has not changed a lot as of 01/2020.

Suggested actions

No one predicts the market correctly and consistently. Otherwise there are no poor folks. Moving the risky investments such as most stocks to cash too early would miss the potential profits. Moving it too late would risk the loss of your stocks.

Your actions depend on your risk tolerance. If you are conservative such as a retiree, you may want to have a larger portion of your investments in lower risk such as CDs and bonds. You can take one of the following three actions or combine all of the three actions.

1. When the market turns to technically unsound, it is time to move your stocks to cash. The market timing indicators may give false signals. In this case, the indicator would tell you to move back to stocks. Most likely you do not lose much except dealing with the consequences of taxes in non-retirement accounts.
2. Move a portion of your risky investments into cash, laddered CDs and/or short-term bonds. Again, the size of the portion depends on your risk tolerance.
3. Use stops. The sell orders would be changed to market orders when the stocks dip below prices specified by you. I prefer to use SPY or other ETF to determine the market direction. Some sectors and some stocks move faster than others. In one crash, my energy stocks were still profitable while the market was tanking. Eventually these energy stocks caught up and fell fast. Today's highly profitable stocks are FAANG stocks as a group.

I propose and prefer 'manual stop orders' to prevent market manipulation. However, usually large ETFs cannot be manipulated easily. Manipulators try to profit from your stop orders. Set a stop order price in your `mind. When the stock falls to that specified price, sell it via a market order.

My friend confirmed my "manual stop order":

"High-frequency trading via Algo Trading Strategy can see exactly where pre-set trailing stops are and sweep across them (play them) like strings on a violin. Pre-set a trailing stop and it is bound to be triggered because Algo hunt them down. Then watch the market rip higher."

Analysis: Fundamentals and Technical

It consists of Fundamental Analysis and Technical Analysis. The former measures how expensive the current market is and the latter measures the trend of the market.

Many metrics were obtained from Finviz.com as of 9/22/2018 while others are obtained from other websites. With the exception of Fidelity.com, all websites described here are free and readily available. It also serves as a guide on how you can do your own market timing especially after a few months.

The following chart uses SPY to represent the market of the top 500 stocks. It is market cap weighted. It means the higher the market cap the stock, the higher percent of the stock is represented in the index. It turns out most are riskier FAANG stocks.

Enter Finviz.com in your browser and enter SPY. I am not responsible for any errors.

Indicator	Pass	Current Value	Indicating
• Technical			
Death Cross[1]		SMA-50 = 2.3% & SMA-200 = 6.3%	Pass
Technical Analysis: 350 SMA%[2]	>0	Price above the SMA-350.	Pass
RSI(14)	<70	61	Pass
Duration (yr.)	<5	10	Fail
		Overall	**Pass**
• Fundamental			
Valuation			

P/E[3]	<15.7	25.4	High by 62%. Fail.
Shiller P/E[3]	<16.6	33.5	High by 102%. Fail
P/B[3]	<2.78	3.52	High by 27%. Fail.
P/S[3]	<1.50	2.33	High by 55%. Fail.
Oil price	30-100	70.71	Pass
Interest rate[6] T-Bill 1 months[7]	<5	2.05	Pass
T-Bill 3 months[7]	Yield	2.18	
T-Bill 30 years[7]	Curve	3.20	Pass
Flow to Equity[4]		-3.371M	Fail
Flow to bond[4]		7.206M	
Corporate debt/GDP[8]	<40	45%	High by 13%. Fail.
USD[5]		Strong	Fail
Gold		High	Fail
Bubble		Several	Fail
Market experts		Fear long term	Neutral
Politics		Trump	Fail
Misc.		Trade war	Fail
		Overall	**Fail**

[1] This is the market timing technique without using a chart.

[2] I tried to use SMA-400% to reduce false signals without success.

[3] Get it from http://www.multpl.com/ Same as CAPE.

[4] Get it from https://www.ici.org/research/stats. It is based on 09-12-18. "Flow to Equity" is based on domestic ETF estimate. Treat it as two phases in moving to equity. First phase of moving excessively to equity indicates the market is peaking. The second phase indicates the market is plunging when flow of equity is excessively negative.

[5] Global corporations will suffer in profits converted back to USD and hard to sell to foreign countries. [4] Get it from the above link.

[6] Rising interest is bad for corporations and high-ticket products, but good for lenders.

[7] Get it from https://www.treasury.gov/resource-center/data-chart-center/interest-rates/Pages/TextView.aspx?data=yield based on 09/21/18

[8] With the low interest rate, it may not be that critical. Corporations take advantage of the low interest rate.

Overall

Overall, technical is fine as the market is making new highs. Many aggressive investors exit the market on technical indicators only as the over-valued market could linger on for a long term such as from 2009 to 2017 so far.

Overall, fundamental is not sound. The increasing market price also is decreasing the fundamental metrics such as P/E, P/B and P/S. It is bad unless there is reason to support such as the fast earnings growth in 2009.

Many metrics are deteriorating

RSI(14) is getting closer to 65 (a passing grade specified by me).

Inverse yield curve (1.5 vs. 2.33) is about 61% apart from my interpretation and calculation. It is not a warning now but we should keep an eye on it. Most market crashes have occurred when it is 0% or negative. The theory is that in a normal case the short-term interest rates should be lower than the long-term interest rate.

Another source calculates it is 1.1% and that is very close to inversion since the last recession. From MarketWatch, the 30-year fixed interest rates is 4.66% and 1-year rate is 3.96% giving an inverse yield curve 18% apart, which is quite alarming.

Mathematically incorrect, today's full employment is at 4%. Most recessions are closely preceded by troughs in unemployment and the reverse for economy recovery.

GDP growth has been predicted from 1.8% to 3%. The 3% is from the White House for their obvious purpose. I predict it will pop up due to meeting the tariff deadlines, tax cuts and spending increases. It will then be declining to 2%. A healthy US economy should maintain 3% without special factors such as excessive immigration.

We have record debts: investors' margin, corporate debt and Federal debt. These are bubbles going to burst. Federal debt / GDP is about 95% (https://fred.stlouisfed.org/series/gfdegdq188S) today. It does not predict the market performance as this ratio was 53% and 55% before the last two market crashes. It will affect the long-term performance of the economy when we have to service the huge national debt.

We do have 10 years of stock growth at the expense of record Federal deficit. Thanks to President Obama from investors and no thanks from next generations who have to pay back our national debt. It is overdue for a correction. Hopefully it is not a crash which has an average loss of about 45%. We did have two recent corrections losing more than 10%: 2011-12 EU debt crisis and 2014-16 oil crash. The oil price has been rising from $30 per barrel to today's $70. It is still a long way from my warning of $120.

Potential triggers
Trade wars with China, Canada or EU will be the strongest trigger. Our most profitable companies are virtually all international companies. They need fair trade to prosper.

The other trigger is the possible impeachment of President Trump.

Check the validity of our charts
It seems some metrics vary. It could use after hour trading. It could be the "Days" may be "Sessions" – calendar day is different from trading session. I selected 10 years for most of the charts and StockCharts let me select only 5 years.

Here is a list of sites for charts.
https://www.stocktrader.com/2013/12/10/best-free-stock-chart-websites/
These are the three sites I use a lot: Fidelity (customers only), StockCharts and Finviz.com (missing some metrics).

As stated before, SPY may not be the best to represent the market. I prefer an ETF for 1,000 stocks and weigh the stocks evenly (i.e. not according to the market cap). Google "market timing 2020 (or current year)" for more expert info. Here is one.

Mid-year update

Basically nothing significant has changed recently: The market is fundamentally unsound and technically sound after the recent rally. The only update is our national debt is skyrocketing. Today's "Debt/GDP" is similar to the market height in 2000 and we know what happened afterwards. That's why Buffett has accumulated a lot of cash now.

Even with the unlimited QE (i.e. printing money excessively), the high inflation and market crash predicted by many experts have not been materialized so far. This is my third prediction in "Disaster of 2020". The status of USD as a reserve currency will be shaken; I do not know when, as I do not have a time machine.

Why the market keeps going up while the economy is going down? The Fed has provided a lot of cash and the cash is chasing a fixed number of assets such as gold and stocks. It is the simple, proven theory of demand and supply. It will continue for a while as long as there is unlimited supply of money. At some point, it will pop. At that time, it could lead to a long recession, unless the economy improves as it did in 2009. The smart Fed chairman knows how it will harm the country by excessively printing money. However, he has to obey his boss who is seeking for reelection.

I expect we are in a prolonged period of low interest rates and even negative interest rates. When the rates are negative, our Treasury bonds are no longer marketable. The foreign central banks including China would dump our national debts if it has not been already started. The economy is dressed up nicely in an election year. Giving us free money is the easy way to buy votes, but the long-term effects are very harmful.

Using cheap money to buy back the company's stock would boost the stock price and hence make the management wealthier. It is a false sense of the stock value. When the company cannot pay back the debt obligations, the company would go bankrupted. If the U.S. were a company, she has gone bankrupted already.

As of 6/15/2020, QQQ (representing NASDAQ stocks) has been up 11% YTD and it is far better than DIA (representing DOW stocks) and SPY (representing the 500 large stocks in the S&P Index and losing about 5% YTD). QQQ has a lot of tech stocks while DIA has a lot of losers including Boeing. Most FAANG stocks are making record highs and QQQ is market cap weighed.

Most of the ETFs on chips have been up more than 40% in a year. I bought Amazon and two chip ETFs. I use trailing stops to protect my portfolio. Huawei is buying a lot of U.S. chips in the 120-day relaxed period. In September this year and if there is no extension, I would sell these chip ETFs fast.

I have used the strategy described in my book "Profit from the recovery of the pandemic" to take advantage of this volatile market. I used 5% as the threshold and I had too few trades; now I changed to 3%. Expecting a market crash, I weigh more on contra ETFs. As described in the same book, I bought a lot of contra ETFs, GLD and the stock of a gold miner. It is for insurance. ETFs on oil is my big mistake.

If the U.S.D. loses the status of reserve currency (not likely soon), it would bring prolonged depression and high inflation in the U.S. In this case, it is safer to invest in real estate, precious metals and profitable companies than in CDs and bonds that would lose values due to inflation.

Check out many articles on the status of the current market. Many have opposing views, so you have to make your own decision. In any case, play it safe with stops. Here is one article from MarketWatch.com.

Canary warning?
When I was working on my new book "Best stocks to buy for 2021" on Dec. 10, 2020, I found something really strange. I have never rejected so many stocks that have Fidelity's Equity Summary Score higher than 9. I rejected them as there were a lot of dumping from the insiders. Insiders know their companies better than most of us. Is it the canary telling us the market is over-valued?

Initially the following stocks have been screened by my value screens. Buy any one of the following stocks, **only** if you have good reason(s).

Symbol	Fidelity Score	Insider Purchase
BCC	9.9	-24%
GPI	10.0	-17%
HEAR	10.0	-75%
HIBB	9.4	-30%
HVT	9.5	-37%
HZO	9.5	-27%

How can HEAR score a perfect 10 while the Insiders' Transaction is -75% (I treated -2% is normal). The analysts must be wrong this time, or they believe the market will continuously make new heights. Will update the performance results later to see who is wrong.

A correction or a crash?

In Dec., 2018, the S&P500 is about 15% down and a crash is about 45% down.

If a crash is coming, there should be additional 30% down. If it is a correction (15% average), then we have it already. Should we pick up bargains now? Or, are they bargains? It is a trillion-dollar question.

We need a trigger for a market crash like the financial crisis in 2008 and the internet bubble in 2000. Besides the record-high margin debt, the possibility of Trump's impeachment and a trade war, I do not see any.

Filler: CIA mistook it as a missile silo in China.

6   Why the market fluctuates

The following chart uses SPY (simulating the market) with SMA-350 for the year of 2020 using Fidelity's charting function. It will be used to demonstrate how SMA-350 worked for 2020; the dates may be several days off. This article is written on 1/1/2021.

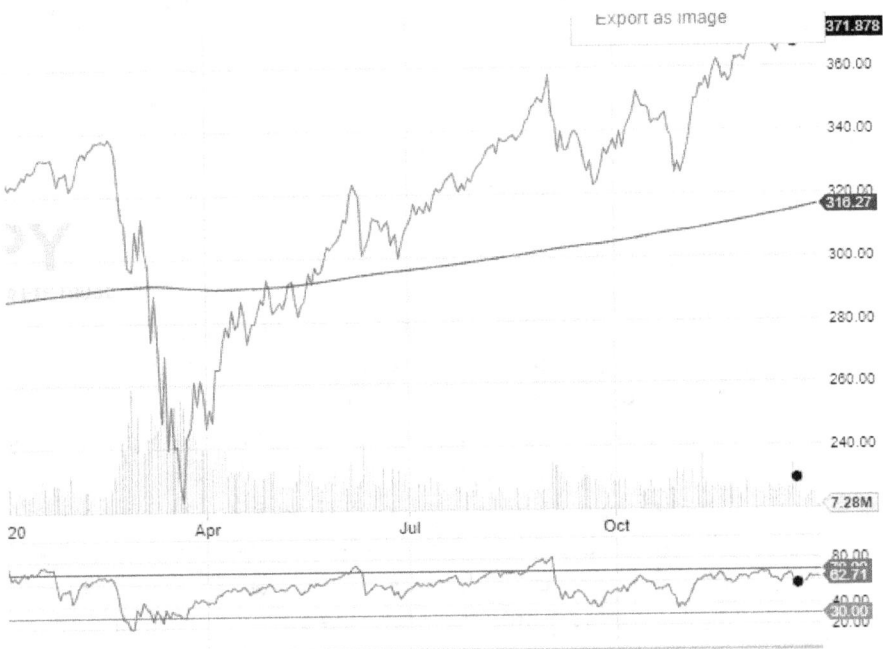

Market Timing

SMA-350 (Simple Moving Average for the last 350 sessions), described in one of my books, worked fine in 2020. It told us to exit the market on about 3/11/2020 and return on about the beginning of June. There were two false signals (on about 4/28 and 5/8) that told you to exit but return to the market shortly.

The other indicators are RSI(14) and P/E. Fidelity's chart uses 80 for overbought and 30 for under-bought for RSI(14). The market has been over-priced for a long while. In this case, technical analysis (SMA-350 I used in my example) works better than fundamental (P/E as one of the metrics); It has been sold for the entire 2020.

Why there is a big drop in late March and why it comes back

The trigger is the pandemic.

The market came back for many reasons:
- We understood the pandemic better.
- A lot of money in the sideline.
- The government supplies more money by printing it excessively.
- The government lowers the interest rate (almost to zero).

2021 prediction

It is quite hard to predict the market. Here are my thoughts. The market is not rational (fundamentally speaking).

For:

- The government keeps on excessively supplying money.
- With easy credit, the rising housing market leads to many profitable sectors such as furniture.
- Due to easy credit and recovering, many companies buy back their own stocks.
- Low margin interest rate usually boosts the stock market.
- If the vaccines can control this pandemic, many sectors will recover. As I demonstrated before, we have to wait one more year for some sectors such as airlines, restaurants and cruise lines.
- Trade war with China could be reduced under Biden.

Against:
- The pandemic has not been stopped.
- Unemployment is breaking previous record.
- Small businesses continue to go bankrupt.
- Complete decoupling with China.
- The government tools do not work anymore such as lowering interest rate.
- Super inflation is due to ample supply of money chasing a fixed amount of assets (stocks for example). The status of the USD as a reserve currency would also be shaken.

As in any market, there are two camps opposite to each other. Need to watch the market like a hawk and take actions accordingly (talk to your financial advisor first). I expect the plunge would cause the market to lose about 40% if it happens.

Stage 2 & 3: Find & evaluate stocks

My steps to trade stocks

This Stage only describes the following #1 and briefly #2.

1. Search for valued stocks (from the proven screens).
2. Evaluate the screened stocks by:
    a. Fundamental Analysis.
    b. Intangible Analysis.
    c. Qualitative Analysis.
    d. Technical Analysis.
3. Sell stocks.

As everything in life, there is no guarantee this book will always make you money. However, the chance of success will be substantially improved especially when you practice on all the ideas presented in this book. Start with paper trading first in this stage.

Chapter 6 demonstrates some screens (used to searching stocks) are better than others in certain market conditions. You should have several screens and keep track of their recent performances.

This Stage is for learning investing and testing out some of the basic concepts. This stage gives you a foundation to the next stage that will use real money in trading stocks.

Continue market timing and trading ETFs as described in Stage 1. Do not use real money in buying stocks using what you've learned in this stage as you're not ready to compete with the professionals.

Beside stock research

In this stage, you should enjoy the better things in life such as owning your own house and taking nice vacations. A trip to Washington DC should not cost a lot but it is fun, memorable and a great learning experience especially if you have children. Buying a fancy car is consumerism and buying a decent house is an investment. Stick with investments.

1   Finviz.com screener

You should use fundamental metrics for fundamental stocks, growth metrics for growth stocks, momentum metrics for momentum stocks, or a combination. Basically you want to keep the fundamental stocks longer so the market would realize their values.

Finviz.com provides a screening function incorporating both fundamental and technical metrics and is one of the best free sites. Bring up Finviz.com in your browser and select screener. You have 4 tabs: Descriptive, Fundamental, Technical and All. It has the following features:

- The criteria specified can be saved but the number is limited.
- The searched stocks can be saved in a portfolio (for paper trading and performance monitoring).
- Technical indicators.
- For an extra fee, you can have a historical database. This would help you to test your strategies. The historical database is quite limited for some technical parameters only.
- Some advanced technical indicators work well especially useful in momentum trading.
- Use technical patterns. My favorites are Head and Shoulder and Double Bottoms (Peaks).
- Combine fundamental metrics and technical metrics to narrow down your selection.
- Combine fundamental metrics and technical metrics to narrow down your selection.
- Add Insider Trans (> 5% for me), Short Squeeze (> 20%), etc. for specific purposes.
- Candlesticks is hard to master. You need to read a book dedicated to it.

http://www.investopedia.com/terms/c/candlestick.asp
https://www.youtube.com/watch?v=FsqoV1aVrUc&list=WL&index=56

Finviz's screener lacks the following features:

- Stocks with prices trending up in the last several weeks (such as increasing X% in the previous week).

- Using exponential moving averages that supposedly have better predictive power than simple moving averages for momentum investing.
- Selecting ranges such as selecting all three major exchanges and market cap ranges.
- P/E for an ETF. It can be obtained from other sources such as ETFdb.com.
- When the earnings (E) is negative, you may have the wrong values for P/E and the metrics using E. For example, if you want stocks with P/E less than 20, the screener returns you stocks with negative earnings.
- Combine fundamental metrics and technical metrics to narrow down your selection.

All of these missing features can be worked around. The paid version may provide better functions.

Links:

Investopedia.
http://www.investopedia.com/university/features-of-Finviz-elite/other-chart-features.asp

How to scan using Finviz (YouTube).
https://www.YouTube.com/watch?v=aQ_0FTg9Cfw
https://www.youtube.com/watch?v=tHtovnCY6uY&list=WL&index=96 (Recommended)

Finviz's screener tutorial.
https://www.youtube.com/watch?v=glMtwB7OVf4&list=WL&index=56

Swing trading
https://www.youtube.com/watch?v=M8sNMhPJINU&list=WL&index=55

Screening using technical indicators (YouTube).
https://www.YouTube.com/watch?v=RZRP2NeSX0s

A screener example

The following is an example. Fine tune the selection criteria according to your personal criteria and risk tolerance.

- Bring up Finviz.com from your browser. Select Screener, the third tab. As of 3/24/2015, we have 7066 stocks.

- For illustration purposes, we would like to find stocks with double bottoms, a positive technical indicator. Select the Technical tab. Select Pattern and then Double Bottom. Now we have 257 stocks.

- Select the Fundamental tab that is next to the Technical tab. Select Forward P/E and then select "under 20". Now, we have 86 stocks.

- Select Debt/Equity less than .5. Now, we have 45 stocks. Some industries such as utilities are traditionally high in debt, so you can use 'less than 1'.

- Select EPS growth Q-to-Q over 10%. Now, we have 19 stocks.

- Select the Description tab. Select Country to USA. Now, we have 17 stocks.

- Select Price > 1. Select Avg. Volume "Over 100K". Select Float Short "Under 10%. Select Analyst Recs. "Buy or better". Now we have 9 stocks.

  Now we can evaluate them one by one using Fundamental Analysis, Intangible Analysis, Qualitative Analysis and Technical Analysis. The purpose of screening is to filter the 7000 stocks to a small number (9 stocks in this case).

Skip the stocks that have the Earnings Date within 2 weeks. If you already have too many stocks in the same industry, skip that stock. You can save the screen when you have registered with Finviz.com. It is free. Check the performance of your selections after 3 months or so.

Other sources

Paper trade and check the actual performance before investing your money. Many popular screens provided by many sites worked before but may not work now. It could be too many folks using the same strategy. Hence it is important to check the current performances of the screen you are using. For yardstick, use SPY or similar ETF that simulates the market. Here are some sources beside Finviz.com.

Your broker

Most broker sites have screen functions. Some have screens to simulate what a specific guru such as what Warren Buffett would buy.

IBD (a subscription service)

From my check on the IBD 50, they're good in the last 10 years, but not that good in the last 5 years – the victim of their own success? They provide stocks from their screens. Most screens are for momentum stocks and large caps. Here are the updated days for specific lists as of this writing.

Stocks Group	Published
Sector Leaders	Daily
Stock spotlight	Daily
Top World	Daily
IBD 50	Mon. and Wed.
Weekly Review	Fri.
Big Cap 20	Tue.

You may want to check out individual stocks with Stock Checkup and then analyze them again. The following are good parameters: Composite Rating, Industry Ranking (finer and better than Sector Ranking) and Relative Price. Understand their parameters and apply accordingly - the same for most other vendors.

IBD prefers large and growing companies with institutional ownership. Some of their parameters may not make sense for small, value and/or turn around companies.

Common parameters

Different styles of investing use different parameters for screening stocks. Here is my suggested parameters in using Finviz.com. Vary them to your risk tolerance and market conditions. Finviz.com is not complete in all functions, but it could the best free screener that incorporates both the fundamental and the technical criteria. The first table is for Value and the next one for Growth. The last one is for finding stocks that the institutional investors are trading.

Screening value stocks

Value Screens	Common	Penny	Micro Cap	Dividend
General				
Market Cap (M)	>500 M	<50 M	50 -200 M	+Mid(>2B)
Price	>5	< 5	1-15	>5
In all 3 Exchanges	In	Not In	Most are In	In
Avg. Volume	>100K	>5K	>10K	>100K
Country	USA	USA	USA	USA
Dividend%				>3%
Float Short	<10%	<10%	<10%	<10%
Analyst Rec	Buy or +	Buy or + if avail.	Buy or +	Buy or +
Fundamental				
Forward P/E	<20	<20	<20	<25
ROE	>10	>10	>5	>15
QQ earning	>0			>0
QQ sales	>0			>0
PEG	<1	<1	<1	<1.2
Payout%				20-50%
P/S	<10	<10	<10	<10
Technical				
Price above 200 SMA	Yes	Yes	Yes	Yes
RSI(14)	< 70	< 70	< 70	< 70

There may be no analysts or very few following penny stocks and micro-cap stocks. QQ is quarter to quarter.

Screening Growth Stocks

Growth Screen	Common	Technical	Momentum
General			
Market Cap (M)	>50	> 1,000	>500
Price	>1	>10	>5
Exchanges (Major 3)	In	In	In
Avg. Volume	>50K	>200K	>100K
Fundamental			
Forward P/E	<30	<30	<30
Return of Equity	>5	>0	>0
QQ earning	>10%	>15%	>20%
QQ sales	>5%	> 5%	>10%
PEG	<1	<1	<1
Analyst recs.	Buy or +		
Technical			
Price above 200 SMA	Yes	Yes	
50 SMA	Yes	Yes	Yes
RSI	< 75	< 75	

Short-term trends are important for momentum stocks.

Explanation

The above are suggestions only. Adjust them to your personal preferences and risk tolerance.

- Finviz screener lacks ranges, such as market cap and multiple of exchanges. Most Finviz's parameters do not have a range option such as Exchanges, so you need to run the screen three times, one for each of the three major exchanges.

- Average Volume. When the price of the stock is less than $3, double the average volume requirement. In most cases, 10K is quite acceptable to me. When the volume is small, you may have to pay more (a.k.a. spread) to trade.

- There are many fundamental metrics such as Debt/Equity and Price/Free Cash Flow that are not included here, but they should be included in your further evaluation. Each industry sector has different thresholds. For example, the P/S is very different for a supermarket rather than a high-tech company. Compare the company to the average value of the companies in the same sector. Many sites including GuruFocus.com and Fidelity.com have the average values displayed.

- For momentum stock, you can ignore most of the fundamentals and concentrate on the price trend such as SMA-20% (Simple Moving Average for the last 20 trade sessions) and SMA-50%. The higher the percent, the higher it is away from its own average. You do not want to hold momentum stocks too long (max. 3 months unless the momentum is still uptrend); personally my max. is 1 month.

- For growth stocks, ensure the PEG (P/E growth), quarter-to-quarter earnings and quarter-to-quarter sales are above the averages in its own sector and/or the market.
- Technical analysis favors large cap stocks with large volumes. I prefer stocks with positive earnings and they are fundamentally sound.
- When the SMA-20%, SMA-50% and SMA-200% are all positive, they should be in an uptrend.
- RSI(14) indicates whether the stock is oversold (>65) or under bought (<30). The range is my suggestion only.
- You may want to check out your strategies using a virtual account from your broker.

A general guideline for Institutional investors

Criteria	Value
Description	
Relative Volume	Over 2 M
Country	USA usually
Institution Ownership	Over 50%
Technical	
SMA-200	>10%
Volatility	Week – Over 3%
RSI(14)	>40%
Fundamental	
Market Cap	>1B
ROE	>10%

- Again, these are my suggested metrics. I prefer USA companies and many are global companies. If you use foreign countries, ensure they are larger companies and/or in countries that have regulations similar to our SEC's.
- For value investors, select Forward P/E less than 20 (25 for high-tech companies) and their Earnings are positive.
- Check out how many analysts are following the stocks that you are interested in.

To illustrate, I find 12 stocks. I narrow them down to 3. First, I skip all stocks that already have had more than 10% rise recently. They may have risen too high already.

Select profitable stocks with forward P/E less than 25. "Debt/Equity" is less than .5 (50%). Then, ROI is higher than 25%. Stop when you have reached the optimal number of stocks (3 for me in this example).

If you find too many stocks, tighten the criteria and vice versa. Save the criteria and the selected stocks in a portfolio for paper trading.

Filler: Irresponsible is my best defense

I told my date that I would not be responsible after the second drink due to the lack of an enzyme.

Filler

Starbucks is being sued for too many ice cubes in the ice coffee. If he wins, he would sue MacDonald's, Burger King... and be a billionaire. Why did I not think of this? The lady won for the spilling of hot coffee. The jury did not know that eventually we had to pay for all of these and made the lawyers rich. Too many unproductive lawyers makes it tough to operate a business including small businesses. In many countries besides the U.S., the one who sues and loses has to pay for court expenses.

2   Finviz's parameters

Most metrics are described in Finviz (via Help), Investopedia and/or Wikipedia and my chapters on P/E and fundamental metrics if available. We use the metrics for screening stocks and then evaluating the screened stocks.

The following are my personal comments and why I feel some metrics are more important than the others. Personally, I divide the metrics into fundamentals and technical, which are more important for long-term investors and short-term investors respectively.

Compare the ratios to the companies in the same sector (industry) and also its averages from the last few years (5 preferable) from many other websites such as Fidelity.

From your browser, enter Finviz.com. Enter a symbol (I used ABEO for discussion). A chart is displayed with the prices and volumes for the last eleven months. SMAs (Single Moving Average) are displayed sometimes with other technical indicators. Intraday, Daily and Weekly options are available for day traders, short-term traders and long-term traders respectively.

Besides the chart and the metrics described next, it describes what the company does, analysts' recommendations (I prefer Fidelity's Equity Summary), insiders' trading and articles that are good for intangible and qualitative analysis. Many free websites such as Yahoo!Finance may provide a list of articles about the company.

"Financial Highlights and Statements" are materials for more in-depth analysis and they were more important decades ago when most financial ratios had not been calculated for you. It is important for investors with good knowledge in financial accounting. The current version also includes basic financial statements and cash flow for the current (TTM) and the last two years.

A section on Insider Trading is also included. Do not be alarmed when insiders dump small quantities of the stocks. Buying large quantities (e.g., insider transaction more than 5%) at prices close to the market price could be favorable news.

The following metrics are roughly based on the flow of Finviz from top to bottom and left to right. I skip those metrics that I believe are not too important. You can also place your cursor on the metric to retrieve the description from Finviz. Some metrics are left blank to indicate they are not applicable (zero, negative or not available). For example, the Debt/Equity of YRCW in 1/2019 is blank (same as null) due to its negative Equity. From Yahoo!Finance at the time of writing, it has a total debt of 888M.

- **Index**. Most of us trade stocks in the three major exchanges in the USA. Stocks listed over-the-counter are too risky for most of us. Skip the stocks in local exchanges and foreign exchanges unless you are an expert on these stocks and/or have insightful (not insider) information. I screen the stocks and then ignore the stocks that are not in the Dow, NASDAQ and Amex. Other screeners may let you select a group of exchanges.

- **Market Cap** (MC). To me, stocks below 50M are risky even though they could be very profitable. Ensure the Avg. Volume is at least 10,000 shares and / or your order is less than 1% of the average volume. Some small stocks are controlled by the owners and have small volumes. In this case you cannot sell your stock easily.

  Float = Outstanding shares – Insider shares.

  Usually, Float does not matter as they are typically the same. However, it does for small companies with large insider shares. Most of these owners do not want to sell their family businesses and hence they reduce the chance of being acquired entirely or partially for good prices. In this case, you may have to hold this stock for a long time or you sell it at a very unfavorable price.

- If **Forward P/E** (a.k.a. Expected P/E) is not provided, use the P/E which is based on the trailing last 12 months (TTM). Alternatively, calculate the E by using the E from P/E and multiplying it by its growth rate. It may not be seasonally adjusted. I prefer using Forward P/E as it provides a better predictability power to me.

  Finviz.com leaves the P/E blank (same as null) if the earnings are negative. In this case, I would check out Yahoo!Finance's EV /

EBITDA, which also considers taxes, cash and interests. The blank condition is similar to some metrics such as when the asset is negative (they seldom occur).

Earnings Yield is equal to E/P. I call it True Earnings Yield for EBITDA / EV. It is easier to understand. Compare Earnings Yield or True Yield to the annual dividend yield of a 10-year Treasury – with the low interest rate in 2021, skip the comparison.

E/P is easier in screening and sorting the screened stocks. If you use P/E instead of E/P, you need to screen or sort stocks with a clause "P/E > 0".

When the P/E is less than 5, be careful and there may be a reason why it is so low. Many bankrupting companies have low P/Es at one time.

Compare the P/E or Forward P/E with the average P/E for the sector and its average P/E for the last 5 years that are available from Fidelity.com. Some sectors have high P/Es. If the sector is cyclical, the earnings could be affected.

When the prospect of the company is good such as Tesla in 2020, ignore P/E.

- **Cash / share**. It is used to calculate Pow P/E and Pow EY when EV/EBITDA for the stock is not available. To illustrate, if the stock is $10 and it has $10 cash / share without debt (i.e., Debt/Equity = 0), most likely it is underpriced as you can get the whole company for nothing. You should find out why the price is so low. It could be the market ignoring the stock, or there is a serious event happening such as a major lawsuit.

- **Dividend %** is useful for income investors. The payout ratio should not be more than 30% except for matured companies. Most developing companies plough back the profits into research and development, and hence they do not pay dividends.

- **Recs**. Select stocks with 1 or 2. Do not base your stock selection on this recommendation alone. There have been many bad recommendations that could cost you a fortune in losses. Use Fidelity's Equity Summary Score instead.

- **PEG** is a measure of the growth of P/E and hence a growth metric. It is similar to P/E, but it takes the expected earnings growth rate into account. The lower value is better as long as earnings are positive. If earnings are negative, then the reverse is true. It is a defect in using P/E and PEG and that's why I recommend EY (Earnings Yield) and EYG, earnings yield growth.

  If there are two companies with the same P/E, the one with a better PEG ratio is better. If two companies have the same E/P, the company with higher Earnings Growth (EPS Q/Q) would be better for similar logic.

- **P/B**. Book value (= Total Assets − Total Liabilities) may not include intangible assets such as patents. Do not trust it 100%, so is ROE which is based on the book value. Negative equity is possible when Total Liabilities is more than Total Assets. This popular metric is outdated for most matured companies as it is now made up of more intangible assets including patents, management, the quality of their employees, brand names, market share, partners, free cash flow and customer base.

- **P/S**. If two companies are unprofitable, this ratio can be used. A retail company such as Walmart is very different from a research company. This metric is only meaningful for stocks within the same sector or specific sectors.

- **P/FCF**. I prefer it to be greater than 0 and less than 50 for value investors. Most metrics can be manipulated easily, but not this one.

- **Sales Q/Q** reduces the seasonal deviation. To illustrate, retail sales for the Christmas season should be compared to the same season in the prior year.

- **EPS Q/Q**. Same as above. I prefer the growth of EPS over Sales. Both of these Q/Q ratios are growth metrics. When a company terminates its unprofitable product(s), its Sales Q/Q could be down but its EPS Q/Q could be up. In 2000, many internet companies had great Sales Q/Qs but negative EPS Q/Qs.

Q/Q comparison (quarter to quarter) takes out the seasonal variations as Sales Q/Q. I prefer both Sales Q/Q and EPS Q/Q increase. When EPS Q/Q increases far higher than Sales Q/Q, it could mean the EPS Q/Q could be temporary such as the oil company when the oil price rockets.

When the company buys its own shares, EPS could be misleading as E is fixed and the number of shares is reduced. In most cases, the fundamentals of the company have not changed.

- Positive **Insider** Transactions are favorable. Sometimes, they are misleading. Need to scroll to the end of the screen and check out more info there. If the transactions are outdated such as 3 months or so ago, and or they are purchases in a similar amount than the sales a while ago, they are not important. Insiders know the company better than us. So is Institutional Transactions as institutional investors move the market.

- Insider Own, Shares Outstanding and Shares **Float** determine the number of shares that are available for trading. A small Float with a high Insider Own limits trading and the stock should be avoided in most cases. Compare your trade position for the stock to the Avg. Volume.

- **Profit Margin**. I prefer it over Gross Margin and Oper. Margin which does not include interest expenses and taxes. When you sell software, the Gross Margin is high as it does not include development, support and marketing, etc. A retail store has low Gross Margin. It all depends on the industry, and hence it is better to compare companies in the same industry.

- **Short Float**. I prefer it to be less than 10%. If it is greater than 10%, the shorters could find something wrong with the company. If it is over 25% (indicating a possible short squeeze), I would check the fundamentals. If they are good, I would buy expecting a short squeeze potential. It is risky but it has been proven to be profitable for me.

- Technical metrics: SMA-20, SMA-50 and SMA-200. Finviz expresses them in convenient percentages. If they are all positive, it means the trend is up. SMA-20 and SMA-50 are a short-term trend and SMA-200 is a long-term trend. If you are a short-term swing investor, stick with the short-term trend and vice versa. The first two are also used as momentum grades. Many long-term investors do not buy stocks when the SMA-200% is negative.

- **RSI(14)**. If it is greater than 65%, it is overbought. If it is under 30%, it is under-bought for me. Some use 5% up or down than mine. Use it as a reference. Most stocks making new heights are always overbought, and many of these stocks keep on rising. I recommend using trailing stops to protect your profit.

- **Beta**. A volatile stock fluctuates a lot. It is good for short-term traders. A beta of 1 means the stock would fluctuate with the market, and be volatile if it is higher than 1. For volatile stocks (higher than 1), the stops should be higher. For example, if your stops are normally 15%, you may want to use 20% or even higher.

- Management performance is measured by <u>ROE</u>. It is also judged by **Analysts' Rec.** and Institutional Ownership (except for small companies). The confidence of their own ability, the company and its sector are measured by Insider Ownership and Insider Purchases.

  ROE = Net Income / Average Shareholder's Equity
  According to Investopedia, a normal ROE for utilities should be 10% while high tech companies should be 15%. Compare this ratio and many other ratios with its peers that are available from Fidelity.

- Avoid all companies that are going to bankrupt at all costs. Debt/Equity, P/FCF, Cash/Sh., P/B, Profit Margin, Forward P/E, Short Float, RSI(14), SMA20% and SMA50 would give us hints. Need to summarize all the info and study many other factors such as obsoleting products (including drugs).

- Unless you have concrete information, do not buy stocks a week or so before the Earnings Date. It is seldom to make great profits when the announcement is better than the expected.

More useful information:

- The price chart. It has a lot of features such as the resistance line. Some charts include technical indicators such as double top (a bearish warning) and double bottom (a bullish sign).
- Description under the symbol. It briefly describes what the company (sector and industry) does and its country of registration. You want to buy a stock within a sector that is trending up. For example, according to Finviz Apple is in the Consumer Goods sector and the Electronic Equipment industry.

  If you do not want to buy foreign stocks, skip it if it is not listed in the US exchange.
- Articles on the company for qualitative analysis.
- Insider trading. Pay more attention to the insider purchases at market prices. Use common sense.
- The last line lets you open Yahoo!Finance and other sites.

Other important sites

Yahoo!Finance.

From Statistics, you can find Enterprise Value / EBITDA. I call it True Yield when I flip them to EBITDA / Enterprise Value.

In case it is not available, I use Earnings Yield. In my spreadsheet without considering the cell designations,

=IF (Earnings Yield = "", True Yield, Earnings Yield)

Fidelity
Compare the P/E of the average PE of the last 5 years. In my spreadsheet for demonstration,

Cheaper By Historically =IF(PE="","",(Avg. of 5-year PE -PE)/Avg. of 5-year PE)

Compare the P/E of companies in the same sector. In my spreadsheet for demonstration,

Cheaper By To the peers =IF(PE="","",(Industry PE - PE)/Industry PE)

Your broker's website

Your broker website should have plenty of tools to analyze stocks. As of Dec., 2018, Fidelity lets you use their extensive research free by opening an account with no position restriction. I describe some of their metrics that should be beneficial to your research.

- Equity Summary Score. Potentially good buy when it is 7 (8 for conservative investors) or higher. With some exceptions, you should avoid or short stocks if the score is 3 or below. The stocks ranking from 4 to 6 could be turnaround candidates if they are supported by good Q/Q Earnings and/or good news.

- The 5-year averages are good yardsticks. For example, in Dec., 2018, C's P/E is about 9 and the average is 14. Hence it is a value buy.

Other sources

If you have other sources (most require a subscription or being a customer), skip the stocks that have one of the failing grades. The exceptions are a new positive development and increased insider purchases.

Vendor	Grade	Fail
Fidelity	Equity Summary Score	< 7
IBD	Composite grade	< 50
Value Line	Proj. 3-5 yr. return. Also, its composite rating	< 3%
Zacks	Rank	5
VectorVest	VST	< 0.7

You may be able to find Value Line and IBD in your library. Try out the free stock reports from your broker first. Finviz and Seeking Alpha should have articles (now fewer free articles from Seeking Alpha) on stocks and earnings conferences, which could have important information after separating from the "welcome" and garbage talks.

Yahoo!Finance has good info. "EV/EBITDA" is better than "P/E" as it considers debts and cash. Most use Earnings from last 12 months, which has poorer predictability than Forward Earnings to me.

When negative values such as Equity in Finviz.com, we need to adjust many related metrics or do not use them at all.

MarketWatch.com has many articles on the market in general and personal investing.

If the stock is close to the Earnings Date (found in Finviz.com), you should avoid trading the stock; as earnings could have a big swing for the stock price. Consult Zacks' ranking which is currently free for individual stocks.

Gurus

It is nice to know how gurus would rate the interested stocks. GuruFocus is a good source. NASDAQ is a simplified version, but it is currently free. Bring up Nasdaq.com from your browser. Select "Investing" and then "Guru Screeners". On the third selection, enter the stock symbol such as THO. Click "Go". You will find how 10 or so gurus would evaluate this stock in theory. Click "Detailed Analysis" for each guru.

Quick and dirty

Many times we need to evaluate a stock fast such as taking action due to some development. Or, when you have over 30 stocks from your screen, you may want to reduce the number by using the following two methods.

Refer to my other article "Simplest way to evaluate stocks". The following should take a few minutes. Bring up Finviz.com and enter the stock symbol.

Using SWKS on 6/10/16 to illustrate, Forward P/E is about 11 (fine between 3 and 25), Debt/Eq. is 0 (fine less than .5), ROE is 30% (fine greater than 5%) and P/PCF is 31 (fine if not negative).

Also, check out Market Cap, Avg. Volume, Dividend, Short Float (fine between 0% and 10%), Country and Industry. Judging from the above, it is a buy.

If you have more time, check out the following: Recom. (Ok if less than 2.5), P/B (fine between .5 and 4), Sales Q/Q (fine if not negative), EPS Q/Q (fine if not negative), Cash/Sh (compare it to Debt/Sh) and Profit Margin (fine >5%). Check some articles described for this stock.

5-minute stock evaluation

It takes even less time than the above "Quick and Dirty". However, I recommend you should spend more time researching stocks.

- From Finviz.com, enter the stock or ETF symbol. Look at the number of reds in metrics. If there are more than greens, most likely it is not a good stock.
- It should be fine if Fidelity's Equity Summary Score is greater than 8.

If you have more time, I recommend you to check the following:

- Check out Forward P/E (E>0 and P/E < 20), Debut / Equity (< 50%) and P/FCF (not in red color).

  If time is allowed, replace Forward P/E with True P/E (same as "EV/EBITDA"), which is available from Yahoo!Finance and other sources.
- SMA20 (or SMA50 for longer holding period). If SMA20 is > 10%, it is trending up.
- It is fine if the Insider Transaction is positive.
- Be cautious on foreign stocks and low-volume stocks.
- If most of the above are positive, it is likely a buy. As in life, nothing is 100% certain.

Links
PEG: http://en.wikipedia.org/wiki/PEG_ratio
Short %:
http://www.investopedia.com/university/shortselling/shortselling1.asp#a
xzz2LNDvpemo
Openinsider: http://www.openinsider.com/
Finviz: http://Finviz.com/
terms: http://www.Finviz.com/help/screener.ashx
Insider Cow: http://www.insidercow.com/
Current Ratio: http://en.wikipedia.org/wiki/Current_ratio
Cash Flow: https://www.youtube.com/watch?v=1v8hRZ36--c
Balance sheet: https://www.youtube.com/watch?v=DZjU0CHKyV4
How to find quality stocks.

http://seekingalpha.com/article/2381395-how-to-identify-quality-stocks-and-is-there-really-alpha-to-be-had

3   Fidelity

Fidelity offers a strong screen function. The most unique feature is incorporating its Equity Summary Score (used to be Analyst's Opinion) and some outside researches such as Zacks and Ford.

From the main menu, select "News and Research", "Screen and Filter" and then "Start a screen".

The following example selects stocks with the following criteria: Security Price (2 to 250), Market Cap. (300 and above), Equity Summary Score (8 and above), Zacks (Strongest) and Ford (Strongest).

It displays the 10 stocks. Research each stock. Read the News about each stock. You may want to use Finviz.com, Yahoo!Finance and other sources to double check.

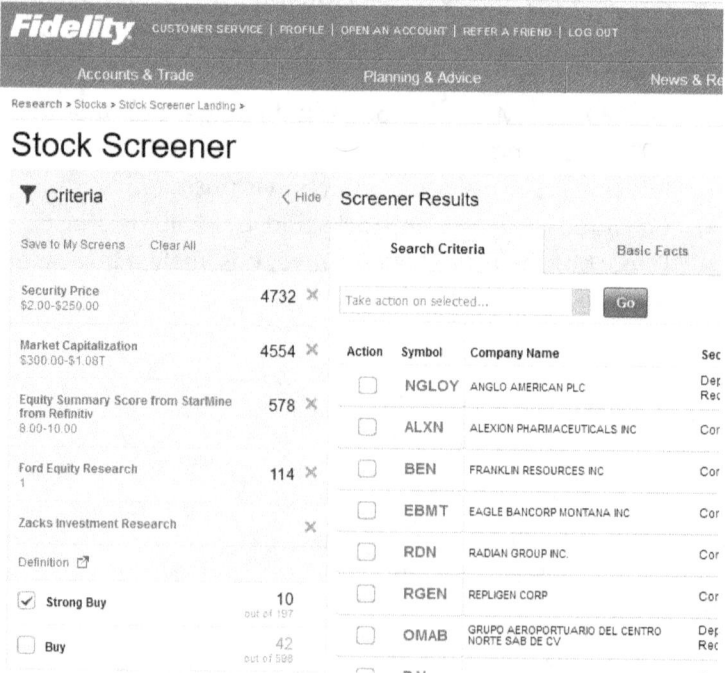

The following describes some of the features.

- Equity Summary Score. It is one of the major metrics I use in my proprietary scoring systems. They are not available to many small stocks. From my limited database in 7/2015 and for short durations, the results are:

Short Term: (7% return for the average)

Metric	Parm. 1	No. of Stocks	%		Parm. 2	No.	%	Predictability
Fidelity Analyst	Buy	150	10%		Sell	279	3%	Good

Long Term: (8% return for the average)

Metric	Parm. 1	No. of Stocks	%		Parm. 2	No.	%	Predictability
Fidelity Analyst	Buy	90	17%		Sell	208	4%	Good

It has its own limits, but they are very minor to me.

First, it does not have a historical database for verifying the screen performance such as the return after a year. However, I do not know any site that provides this function free. To work around this, I save the results in a spread sheet and update the performance.

Secondly, it does not provide many other filter criteria that can be found in other systems such as technical indicators or insider transactions found in Finviz.com. I use other sites for further evaluation.

Most investors should find that this screening is a very good tool and very easy to use.

4   Sectors to be cautious with

There are many reasons to be very cautious when investing in the following sectors. However, Technical Analysis (a.k.a. charting) would give you more hints than the fundamentals for stocks for these sectors. If the big guys are dumping, most likely Technical Analysis (or the simplest SMA-20) would tell you that.

Loan companies/banks

The financial statements do not show the quality of their loan portfolios. Following this advice, you may be able to skip the banks that melted down in 2007. The peak of Citigroup is $550 and several banks went bankrupt.

Many metrics are not relevant for banks such as Debt/Equity and EBIT. The rising interest rate would be good for banks' profits.

Drug (generic is ok)

Understanding the complexities of the drug pipelines, its potential profits for new drugs and the expiration of the current drugs may not worth the effort for most retail investors. In addition, a serious lawsuit and / or a serious problem with a drug could wipe out a good percentage of the stock price. When a drug shows unpromising sign(s) in any trial phase, the stock could plunge and vice versa.

Miners

It is extremely difficult to estimate how much ore (sometimes a miner owns several different types of ores and/or of different grades in the same or different mines) that a company has. It is further complicated by the complexities to extract and transport them. When the total of these costs is greater than its production price, the company will not be profitable. Understanding the market for ore futures is another discipline.

Many mining companies are in foreign countries such as Canada, Australia and countries in South America. Their financial statements of Canada and Australia are more trustworthy than most other emerging countries.

One potential problem of mining companies from many emerging countries is nationalization.

Mining rare earth ore is extremely risky when the profit depends on how China, a major producer of these ores, will price these ores. After China announced the export restrictions on rare earth elements, several non-Chinese companies announced to reopen their mines for rare earths, but few have made any profits as of 2013. Developed countries have stricter environmental regulations.

Coal and eventually oil suffer from the rising use of cleaner energy such as solar and wind.

Insurance companies
Insurance companies profit by:

1. The difference between the total premiums received and the total claims minus expenses in running the company.

2. How well they invest the premiums; you pay your premiums earlier than you may collect from any claims.

They can protect the profits in #1 by restricting claims by natural disasters such as earthquakes and by re-insuring. However, a bad disaster could wipe out a lot of their profits.

Even if the insurance company shows you its investment portfolio, most of us, the retail investors, do not have the time and expertise to analyze it.

Emerging countries (not a sector)
Their financial statements especially from small companies cannot be trusted, and many countries use different accounting standards. Emerging countries are where the economic growth is. I trade FXI, an ETF, rather than individual Chinese companies. I have lost a lot in small Chinese companies due to frauds and politics. To check out whether the stock is an ADR, try ADR.COM (https://www.adr.com/).

Stocks with low volumes (not a sector)
Most likely you pay a high spread to trade these stocks. They can be manipulated easier. I had a hard time trying to sell a stock owned by a few owners.

For simplicity, I trade stocks with the average daily trade volume over 6,000 shares (double it if the price is $2 or less). A better way could be by calculating the percent of your trade quantity / average daily trade volume; it would reduce the effect of penny stocks that have larger volumes due to the low prices.

Good business and bad business

Banking is a good business in a growing economy. My deposit in them makes virtually zero interest, and they loan the same money making 3%. If they are more cautious in loaning, they should make good profits.

Restaurant is an easy business to run, but it is very hard to make good money. With the rising of minimal wages, it will get even tougher. That could be the reason for so many coupons today. The high-end restaurants are doing better due to the rising stock market. The pandemic of 2020 would wipe out a lot of small restaurants.

Retailing is a tough business. Look at the top 10 retailers 15 years ago, I can only find two including Macy's that are still surviving. Most are either went bankrupt or being acquired. Even Macy's was not in good financial shape. Amazon is the killer.

Airlines are a tough business. You can tell by the average increase in fares in the last 10 years. It cannot even beat inflation. They have to charge you for everything. The next frontier charge is the rest room (especially for long-distance flights). Now I understand why they call themselves "Frontier Air". As of 2014, it is quite profitable due to mergers and lower fuel cost. The pandemic of 2020 may be the toughest time for airlines. As of 5/2020, Boeing has many serious troubles and they can only survive with a bailout from the government.

There are several software companies that produce software such as the virus detecting programs and tax preparation software. The customers faithfully buy new versions every year. That's great business.

5   Intangibles

I give a score for each stock I evaluate. Occasionally some stocks with poor scores have great returns and vice versa. In general, the scoring system works. It has been proven statistically and repeatedly from my limited data.
I stick with high-score stocks with some exceptions.

Once in a while I change my scoring system to adapt to the current market conditions. To illustrate, the market bottom phase and early recovery phase of the market cycle favor value more than momentum/growth. Here are some of my recent experiences and strategies:

- I double or even triple my stake on stocks with high scores. In the longer term, they are consistently better winners than the average with some minor exceptions. Besides the score, look at the intangibles described in this article.

- Watch out for the stocks with outrageous metrics such as P/E of 4 or less. It could be a big lawsuit pending, an expiration of some important drugs, etc. Also, be careful with scores in the top 5%. From my statistics they do worse than the average. Their problems may not show up in the current financial statements.

- The technology of a tech company cannot be ignored even though the company's P/E is high, that I set a limit of 25 instead of 20 for other stocks. The value of the company's technology and patents will not be shown in the fundamental metrics except from the insiders' purchases at market prices.

  For example, IDCC rose about 40% in 2 days. There was a rumor that Google was buying the company and/or Apple was bidding on it too for its mobile technology. Charts usually would flag this kind of event. For non-charters, use the SMA-20% from Finviz.com. They could be a little late as the charts depend on rising prices.

- There are more acquisitions during a market bottom (same as early recovery). The companies with good technologies are bargains and the larger companies especially those in the same sector understand their values better than most of us. These potentially profitable companies will not be shown by their scores explicitly. When corporations have a lot of cash or the credit is cheap, they are looking for smaller companies to acquire or invest in. The candidates are usually small, beaten up, low-priced and having valuable intangible assets such as technologies, customer base and/or market share of the industry segment. 2009-2012 was just the perfect environment and the before that was 2003. I had at least one stock in each of these periods and they appreciated a lot.

- The opposite is Netflix, Chipotle in 1/2012 and Amazon in 1/2013. They are overpriced by any measure. However, the mentioned companies are investing in the future. The shorters (not for beginners) are having a tough time making money on them. When their P/Es are higher than 40, watch out. Some could be OK in the mentioned companies, but usually they are not. Do not follow the herd and your due diligence will verify whether they will still go up.

  Use reward/risk ratio. It is based on experiences. To illustrate, if the company has the equal chance to go up 50% and go down 25%, then it is a buy and the reverse is a sell.

- The retail investor just cannot possibly know about some events until they actually happen. For example, ATSC dropped 15% due to losing its second primary customer. Fundamentals cannot predict this kind of event. Charts can signal this event, but usually they are too late unless you watch the chart all day long.

- After a quick run up, TZOO plunged due to missing some negligible earning expectations. It seems the original climbing prices already had the perfect earnings growth built-in.

  I do not understand why a company loses 10% of its market cap when it missed by 1% of the expected earnings. It could be driven up and down by the institutional investors. Evaluate the stock before you act. Acting opposite to the institutional investors could be very profitable for the right stocks. Avoid trading before the earnings announcement dates (about 4 times a year for most stocks).

- The following are not easily found in financial statements: industry outlook, patents, good will, market share, competition, product margins, management quality, lawsuits pending, potential acquisition, pension obligations, advertising icons, etc. That is why we need to read articles on the stocks in our buy list or our purchased stocks.

- The financial data could be fraudulent or manipulated. I do not trust small companies in emerging markets. I have been burned too many times. Check the company names such as foreign names, ADR and their headquarter addresses (from the company profile in most investing sites).

  Earnings can be manipulated with many accounting tricks. A jump in earnings from last year may not be as rosy as it looks. Check the footnotes in the accounting statements. I usually skip financial statements unless I have big purchases in mind as my time in investing is limited.

- Cash flow cannot be easily manipulated. It is good information whether the company will survive or not, but to me it does not prove to be a consistent predictor in my tests, but an important red flag for companies on their way to bankruptcy. Examples abound.

- Repeated one-time, non-recurring and extraordinary charges are red flags.

- Stay away from the companies where the CEOs are over-compensated. As of 7- 2013, Activision's CEO raised his salary by more than 600%, while the stock lost its value in double digits.

- Value stocks. Need to know why they become value stocks (i.e., fewer investors want to own them) even if they are fundamentally sound. For example, there are two primary reasons for the downfall of a supplier to Apple: 1. Apple is declining in sales and 2. Apple is switching suppliers to replace their product. Technology companies are continually building better mouse traps. They could turn around in a year or so with better products.

Conclusion

Buying a stock is an educated guess that its stock price will rise. Fundamentals do not always work, but they work most of the time:

1. When we buy a value stock, we're swimming against the tide. Hence, we need to wait longer (usually more than 6 months) for the market to realize its value. The exception is the Early Recovery phase (see the Market Cycle chapter) and it has faster and larger returns than most other stocks from most other stages of the market cycle.

2. Some metrics are misleading. Book value could be misleading for an established company such as IBM. The image of the cowboy in a tobacco company could be a very important asset that is not included in its financial statement.

3. The market is not always rational.

Afterthoughts

*   Brand names of big companies are one of the most important intangibles. Here is a strategy to buy big companies in a down market. It has been proven that it works. However, do not just buy these companies without analysis.
    http://seekingalpha.com/article/1324041-buying-brand-names-in-a-bear-market-can-make-you-rich

*   The reputation of a company takes a long time to build but a bad incident to destroy in the case of GM such as the delay in recalling the killer switches.

#Filler: Carrie Fisher, another sad American story
Unless drug addiction is part of the culture now as evidenced from the legalization of certain drugs, we're in a permissive society! Brits pushed opium as a nation when they had nothing better to trade. Opium killed millions of Chinese and bankrupted China. When we do not learn from history, we will repeat history. It is another sad story of fame and money and then losing it all. I bet she would be happier in a normal life instead of being born in a privileged class. Same can be said for many celebrities such as Presley, Houston and her daughter. RIP.

6   Qualitative analysis

This is the last analysis to evaluate a stock fundamentally. Then the next is technical analysis which is used to find an entry point (also the exit point) for the stock. The market is not always rational. It also depends on the available of money such as easy credit to pump up the market.

Where quantitative analysis fails and why

I find that some stocks with high scores fail and some stocks with low scores succeed as indicated by my performance monitor. The scoring system still works statistically for the majority of my stocks.

- Reasons why stocks with low scores perform:

  o Oversold. The institutional investors (fund managers and pension managers) dump them first, and then followed by the retail investors. These big boys will buy these stocks back when they reach a certain price range. RSI(14), a technical indicator described in the Technical Analysis article and is available from many sites including Finviz, is useful to detect these oversold stocks.

  o The falling price (P) improves all fundamental metrics that have the stock price such as P/E and P/Sales. However, the trend of the price is down. Improving Forward P/E is usually a good hint.

  o The company has turned around after fixing its problems and/or the market has changed for the better. A new management team could improve profitability such as recalling Steve Jobs for Apple.

  o The current problems have been resolved but not known to the public that could be evidenced by the increase in Insiders' Purchases (from Finviz to start). It includes resolving a lawsuit, a new product, a new drug, or a new big order, etc.

  o Heavy purchases by insiders. The company's outlook is not shown in its financial statements. Sometimes the insiders hide them so they can buy more of their companies' stocks for themselves.

- Reasons why stocks with high scores plunge in addition to the described in the previous discussion:

  o The company's fundamentals and its prices have reached or closed to the maximum heights. They have no way to go but down. It is particularly true when the stock's timing rating is at or close to the highest point. TTWO that I gifted to my grandchildren had been 5-baggers in the last few years before it plunged in 2018.

  o It has reached its potential value (or a target price) and it is time for many investors to take profits.

  o Sector (or finding another stock or sector with better appreciation potential)) rotation, particularly by institutional investors who drive the market.

    o The outlook of the company, its sector and/or the market is deteriorating. Most companies with P/E less than 5 have problems, and you need to find out the reasons why the stocks are so cheap. Via Finviz, check out debt / share (more than 0.5), negative Q-Q Sales, negative Q-Q Profits, and/or outdated products like typewriters.

  o The stock price may be manipulated. There are many reasons to pump and dump the stock. Shorting is not recommended for most investors. However, some experienced shorters make money consistently when they find valid reasons to short stocks.

  o It could be due to a new serious lawsuit, a new competing product or drug, canceling a major order, etc.

  o Downgrade by analysts. They could spot some bad events such as product defects, violations of regulations or accounting errors / frauds. The downgrades are more important than the upgrades that could have conflict of interest.

- o The financial statement had been manipulated. The SEC may ask for an investigation.
- o Does not meet the consensus in earnings announcements, which have been over-acted by many investors.

Qualitative Analysis

We need to do further analysis after the quantitative analysis and the intangible analysis. Check out the company's prospects. Check out the date of the article and any potential hidden agenda items from the author. Older articles may not have much value.

Be careful on 'pump-and-dump' manipulation written by authors with a hidden agenda. It has happened especially on small companies before even SeekingAlpha.com has its share. Here was an article that tells you to sell NHTC. There was another article to tell you to buy ARTX. They fit into this category.

The sources are:

1. Seeking Alpha.
   Type the symbol of the company to read as many articles on the company as you have time for. Today this site and many other similar sites require you to be a paid member. If you cannot find too many good articles, check out the articles from Finviz.com.

   Recently, I read an article on AMD and it said it may have good profits in the next two years with the game consoles. The outlook of a company is not shown by any fundamental metric which are far from favorable.

   Following a well-known writer, I bought IBM without doing my due diligence (my fault). It went down more than 15% quickly. You can learn from my mistakes.
2. Research reports from your broker. If you do not find many, open an account with one that provides such reports. Some subscription services such as Value Line provide such reports.
3. Yahoo!Finance board. Most comments are garbage. However, once in a while you find some great insights. Usually, you cannot find any info from other sources on tiny companies.
4. The most recent company's financial statements. They are usually available from the company's website.

5. 10-Ks from Edgar database (www.sec.gov/edgar). Check out new products and its potential competition, key customers, order backlog, research and development and pending lawsuits.
6. Check out the outlook of the sector the company is in and the company itself.
7. Check out its competitors.
8. Some companies are run by stupid people. I received information via my email saying that my mutual fund account could be treated as an abandoned property. I have been cashing dividend checks every year and why it would be considered as an abandoned property. I called them right away to close my account.

The tall and handsome guy presented articulately how he would turn around JC Penny on TV. I could tell you right away that all his tricks had been tried by other companies such as Sears, and most did not work. The intelligent investor does not care about how handsome, how articulate, how rich his family is and how many advanced degrees from prestigious colleges he possesses. If he does not make sense, do not buy his preaching and his company's stock. [Update. As of 5/2020, J.C. Penny filed for bankruptcy protection. If you had this stock and my book, you would have saved a lot of money minus $10 for my book!]

9. Check out its business model. Some business models do not make business sense and some do. Here are some samples.
- Giving razors makes sense, as the customers have to buy the blades eventually and keep on buying blades for life.
- Supermarket M lowers prices on common merchandise such as Coke and it works. They make money by providing inferior (but profitable to them) products that you cannot compare prices easily such as meat and seafood.

Eventually there will be a supermarket in my area to satisfy me both in price and quality or at least make a good tradeoff.
- Last week it had been brutally hot. I went to a Barnes & Noble's bookstore to enjoy reading the updated books and enjoyed the air conditioning. When there are more free loaders like me than customers, this business model does not work.
- Market dumping works to capture the market. Microsoft used to do it with their new Office and Mail products that could not compete with the established products at the time. Google is

following the same model to dump its equivalent products to compete with Office. Now, Microsoft is taking a dose of the same medicine. As of 2015, Google is not winning.

Amazon.com gives writers (like myself) great deals if you only sell your digital books via them. This model will work so far, as it has captured the self-publishing market today.

#Filler: Why do poor countries remain poor?

One reason is suffering from repeated natural disasters such as earthquakes and hurricanes.

Even though the U.S. has been spending a lot of resources on Puerto Rico, some politicians want to be kings and queens as they do not care about their citizens.

#Filler: One way to evaluate a company

https://www.youtube.com/watch?v=fGVtypWv04Y

7   Manipulators and bankruptcy

If we can avoid bankrupting companies and/or companies losing most of their stock values, our portfolio would be improved substantially. Some companies make bad bets and lose, such as Enron betting on energy futures. Here are some signs of bad situations.

- Foreign companies. I do not have too much luck in developing countries, especially their stocks of small companies. They include China, Ireland and Israel to name a few. However, as of 2019, many large Chinese companies are doing very well.
- When the P/E is too good, find out why. If the P/E is too bad, stay away.
- P/PFC should be greater than 0 and less than 50. Even a healthy cash flow may not be able to service the debt if it is huge. Hence, compare the cash flow to Debt/Equity.
- Altman Z-Score. I prefer a score above 3, a sign not to be bankrupt. However, Z-Score is not designed for financial sectors.
- Beneish M-Score. I prefer a score less than -2.22, a sign that the earnings are not manipulated. Both Z-Score and M-Score are available from GuruFocus.com for a fee.
- Z-Score metrics are: "Working Capital / Total Assets" (A), "Retained Earnings / Total Assets" (B), "Earnings Before Interest & Taxes / Total Assets" (C), "Market Cap / Total Liabilities" (D) and "Sales / Total Assets" (E).
  Z-Score = 1.2 A + 1.4 B + 3.3 C +.6 D + E
- Skip companies with bond ratings less than B.
- New government regulations such as taking out the credit for solar panels.
- Extraordinary profits such as Timber Liquidator and many banks in 2007-2008.
- Accounting manipulation: Excessive buying of stocks to boost Earnings per Share, excessive loans to officers, companies betting on futures such as Enron, too many one-time charges and reinstating the previous earnings.
- Skip thinly-traded stocks especially those stocks with the majority owned by a few owners.

The current financial statements could be the best source to look for them. If you read something you do not understand, be cautious.

We need to consistently monitor our stock holdings and sell them before they lose most of their value. I Recommend use stops.

This is why we need to have a focused investment portfolio of about 10 stocks; the number depends on your time available for investing. To illustrate, I have about 10 stocks with larger investments and about 100 stocks in smaller purchases. I would likely spend more time in monitoring the 10 stocks than the rest.

Mergers

Mergers are usually good for the merging companies to eliminate duplicate corporate functions such as payroll administration and researching on similar subjects.

The company being acquired usually has a high appreciation. I have a screen to search for the potential candidates. The Early Recovery (a phase of the market cycle defined by me) has more of these candidates. Big companies know their values and see good values when these stocks have been beaten in the market.

Then I do an intangible analysis on items that are not available from the financial statements and/or cannot be quantified. They are patents, technologies, research, customer base, the brand name, the barriers to entry, the distribution channels, the competition, the product cycle, the management and the pension obligations.

In 2003 I bought stock in a software company that was acquired by IBM profiting more than double. In the 2008 cycle, I bought ALU at $1 and sold it shortly at 40% profit. I expected Cisco would acquire it as Cisco did not build a network. Cisco and the U.S. did not acquire this valuable technology. In two years, it was acquired by another competitor for more than $3. I need patience.

The company going to be acquired tries to make the financial statements look very rosy. A Chinese company tricked Caterpillar in acquiring it and Caterpillar lost huge in this deal. Even big companies can be fooled. The record mergers in 2015 may not be good for the companies involved judging from the past history. When two losing companies merge, there will be one big loser.

8   Avoid bankrupting companies

Avoid the bankrupting companies at all costs. Here are some hints that a company is going bankrupt:

- I had several companies that had lost most of their stock values. It turns out that most were Chinese companies. I did have some losers from Mexico, Israel and Ireland. I believe most were set up to cheat investors. Most if not all had 'rosy' financial statements. Avoid them, especially small companies in emerging countries.

- Many U.S. companies failed due to fraud, poor management, and/or the management betting wrongly. When the CEO is using the company as his own AMT, or having an extravagant lifestyle, watch out. If they promise you a return doubling the current rate of return of the market, listen to your wise mother: there is no free lunch. Despite so many real examples, still fools are born every day, because greed is a human nature.

- Do not follow the 'commentators' on TV. They have their own hidden agenda which usually is not in your interest.

- Many companies fail due to their lack of ability to pay back their loans. Except for specific industries and situations, avoid companies with high debt (Debt/Equity over 50%). Financial institutions and companies that have high debt in order to finance their products for their customers such as utilities are the exceptions.

- I have a screen named Big Losers beating the market by more than 600% in Early Recovery (a phase defined by me). However, some bankrupt companies are not included in the database which is termed as survivor bias. Hence, the actual result is far worse than the 600%. I still use this screen but skip these companies using the following yardsticks.
    - The companies are usually safe with high Free Cash Flow / Equity and high Expected Profit / Stock Price.
    - The following are red flags: low Free Cash Flow / Equity, high Inventory and high Receivable (esp. relative to its Payable), high P/B (over 30) and high net Debt/Equity (over 1 to 3 depending on the industry).
    - P/PFC should be greater than 0 and less than 50. A healthy cash flow may not be able to service the debt if it is too huge. Hence, compare it to Debt/Equity. Compare the cash flow per year to debt obligations per year.

- New government regulations could bankrupt an industry. What would happen when the U.S. takes out the rebates and subsidies of solar panels? When the U.S. banned solar panels from China, one of my Chinese stocks went bankrupt. Also, the government bailed out bankrupt companies such as Chrysler (that I made a good profit from) and AIG Fannie Mae in 2008.
- Serious lawsuits- Most U.S. companies are required to file this information in their financial reports.
- Obsolete products. Newspapers, retail and similar products would be replaced by the internet. The opposite is new products such as virtual reality products.
- Many companies run out of money during the development phase of the major products. Many are too optimistic in their business plans.
- If you expect the market will recover in 2 years, ensure the company's cash and net income can support their burn rate for at least two more years.
- Many investing sites (most require subscriptions) have safety scores.
- If the Beneish M-Score is greater than -2.22, the company is likely an accounting manipulator.
- Choose companies with Z-Score higher than 3; it is not applicable to financial companies. Both M-Score and Z-Score are available from GuruFocus, a paid subscription. Z-Score does not work for financial institutions.
- Z-Score metrics are: "Working Capital / Total Assets" (A), "Retained Earnings / Total Assets" (B), "Earnings Before Interest & Taxes / Total Assets" (C), "Market Cap / Total Liabilities" (D) and "Sales / Total Assets" (E).
  Z-Score = 1.2 A + 1.4 B + 3.3 C + .6 D + E
- Market timing- It does not always work, but it is far better to follow a proven technique than not. It is far safer to take money out of the market when the market is too risky or is plunging. The big losers are companies that provide non-essential products in a downturn.
- Small companies could be risky but very profitable. Typically, they have a low stock price (less than $5), small market cap (less than 50 M), low sales (less than $25 M) and low institutional ownership (less than 5%).
- Avoid companies when their own bond ratings are not equal to AAA or AA (www.moodys.com).

9   Order prices

Market orders
It is simply trading the stock at the prevailing market price. Place market orders only when it is necessary as stocks price can easily be manipulated especially on stocks with low trading volumes. To avoid manipulations, do not place market orders after hours.

However, in a rising market, many fast-rising stocks can only be bought via market orders. Many winners never take a breather on their way up. In this case, you can only buy the stock via market orders.

Consider bid and ask. A 'bid' is the price a potential buyer would like to buy while the 'ask' is a potential seller would like to sell. Your market price is usually the worst price in either case, but it is a guarantee that you would trade the stock. A large spread would mean that it would take a longer time to use a limit order and/or the trade volume of the stock is small.

In my momentum portfolio on 11/2013, I placed a sell price for GERN far higher than the market price. Surprisingly I sold it for this price making an annualized return of 1,176% for holding it for 21 days. When there are few or no other sellers for the stock, the market price would be the price you set. If I cannot sell it in the next 9 days (30 days is my holding period for momentum stocks), I would set it lower. Update: One year later, GERN lost 29%.

Sensible discounts
I prefer to buy the stock at the price closest to the last trade price (to most it is the market price) via a limit order. I seldom lose buying these orders. Sometimes I use the day's lowest price to buy (or the highest to sell) plus a penny (or minus a penny for sell prices to sell).

My other purchase strategy is using 0.15% or 0.25% less than the current prices for stocks I really want. For some promising stocks, I buy them at almost the market price and then place another order on the same stock at 0.5% less than the last traded price (and sometimes 2% depending on the current market trend).

We all want to buy less and sell at higher prices. However, if the trade price is too far away from the current market price (such as

5% from the market price), these trades may never be executed. I have had a long list of buy orders that were not executed and turned out to be big gainers. Learn from my bad experiences.

Use a good discount (such as 10% from the market price) if you believe the market, the sector or the stock will dip by 10%. After you bought the stock, you place a sell order 10% more than the price you paid for it hoping the stock will return to the original price and you pocket 10%. Wishful thinking! However, it has happened to me several times primarily due to temporary market dips.

It works when there is a correction and/or the stock is very volatile. It is usually within the 5% range to take advantage of these situations, not the 10% as described. For a 10% plunge, it usually is due to some serious problem of the company surfacing. One common reason is not meeting its earnings expectation and in this case it usually continues its downward trend.

Larger discounts on a falling market
During a falling market (or a mild correction), 3% less than the current prices for buy orders may be fine for some stocks (use 5% for volatile stocks). To illustrate, I placed about 10 of these orders over the last two months during a market dip. Most of the orders were filled. When the market is plunging, do not buy any stock.

Caterpillar and Cisco were some of my buys at these discounts. They were in my watch list to buy. Initially these shares often fall even lower as the trend was downward. As of 12/18/12, CAT earned me from 3% and 14% (bought in 6/12 and 7/12) and CSCO bought in 7/14/12 returned about 34%. My original objective: Buy deeply-valued stocks, wait and sell them when the economy returns.

When you predict the market will dip by 5%, set your buy orders accordingly. Again, predictions are just educated guesses. From my experience, they work most of the time but not all of the time.

On the day of the earnings announcement, the fluctuation of the stock is usually high. Check any change in the earnings estimate before the announcement and act accordingly. Zacks is supposed to be a useful tool to predict earnings estimates. Do not leave orders during the earnings announcement dates, which can be found in Finviz. When the earning turns out to be good, the stock price surges and your order will not be executed. When the earnings are bad, the stock price will plunge usually and you most likely over-paid.

Option expiration dates usually cause more volatility. Retail investors do not have to be concerned except you may use wider stops. In theory, dividend days have little effect on the stock price as it will be lowered by the dividend amount.

High volume of a stock could mean opportunity

High volume usually increases the stock price volatility. If the volatility of a stock increases substantially (such as doubling its average daily volume), there could be important news on the company, recommendation changes from a major analyst or trading by the institutional investors. It usually takes the institutional investors a week to trade a stock with their sizable positions.

Many times it is started by the insiders who know about the breaking news of a stock before it is publicized. Some investment services / sites specialize in identifying the increasing volumes on these stocks.

Because day traders do not want to leave any open positions overnight, higher volatility occurs at the end of the day. It is the same on the day (usually on Friday) when the options are expiring.

Monitor your trade prices

You cannot tell whether you are paying a fair price without keeping a record. To illustrate, you're paying 1% less than the market prices in buying stocks. You may have missed buying some winners. If the 1% you saved is smaller than the appreciation of the stocks you would have bought at market prices, then you should adjust the buy prices to 0.5% less than the market price and monitor again.

Market trend makes a difference too. When the market is trending up, buying any stock would most likely be profitable and usually the purchase orders with higher discounts will not be executed.

Follow the same logic on sell orders. Need to have at least 25 stock purchases (and potential purchases) to make the conclusion meaningful. If you do not trade a lot, you will not have enough data to verify. As described, I prefer not to place an order during the earnings announcement dates which can be found in Finviz.com. If you cannot buy the stock, consider to use market order the next day. With most brokers offer no commission trades, the "All or none" option is not valid.

Good prospects

When you find gems especially those stocks that are followed by analysts, buy them at market prices and consider doubling the bet if you are really sure you have a winner. From my super stock screens, I spotted NHTC. I placed several bets and one market order. All of them were NOT executed except with the market order. At the end of the day NHTC is up 18% and my executed order is up 14%. I did not have the best buy but made a good profit. NHTC was on its way to a huge appreciation and I sold it too early. I have earned not to sell a winner and protect the profit with a stop.

Lower the buy for risky stocks (if the beta from Finviz is greater than 1 for example) even if they have good fundamentals.

Quality over quantity

If your time is limited, spend all the time on researching one stock one at a time. However, you need to own at least 3 stocks (more stocks for a large portfolio) for your diversification purposes.

Double your normal purchase position on stocks that look great after the research. For risky stocks that look good, you may want to halve your normal purchase position to cut down on the risk. If you are less risk tolerant, do not buy risky stocks at all. My results are not conclusive on risky stocks but I do get a good sleep.

A recent example

Recently I sold EA with $1 more than my order price but $2 less than the current price of the day, which was the earnings announcement day. I do recommend not placing orders right before the earnings announcement day for the stock. If the earnings are good, you do not get all the profit as in this real example; my broker did get me $1 more. If the earnings are bad, you will not sell it any way. It is the same for buying stocks.

10   Diversification

LTCM, a hedge fund run by smart people, and Isaac Newton both made one serious mistake in investing. They both bet all in one bet and they lost it big. They were the smartest folks on earth but they violated one basic principle in investing: diversification.

Another example is the potato. Irish made good living in their primary crop: potato. When a virus came, they lost all the potatoes and caused the potato famine.

Diversification improves a portfolio's performance in the long run and it reduces risk. Diversification includes other asset class besides stocks such as oil, gold, cash (yes even cash as a safety net to grasp better opportunities ahead), real estate, etc. However, stocks historically produce the best return. In addition, most stocks are quite liquid as it takes a minute to sell them compared to selling a house for example. You can buy other assets such as gold (GLD), money market funds and real estate (via REITs) via the low-cost ETFs.

When an asset is over-valued, it will return to the average historical value with one or two exceptions. Gold is one exception, but it is partly due to the depreciation of USD and the previous prolonged downfall of gold adjusted to inflation.

Simply put, owning 10 to 15 good stocks with less than three stocks in the same sector (which have to be good sectors to start with) achieves diversification goal for most. When one sector crashes, you still have two more good sectors.

Every one's situation is different:

- Depends on your wealth and your age.
  For younger folks with limited wealth (less than $50,000 to invest), a portfolio of 3 stocks (preferably most in ETFs) in different sectors or one diversified ETF could be enough. Your objective in investing is saving money for a down payment for a house, paying your loans including college loans and/or improving your earning power by taking classes.

  Retirees may want to maintain a larger percentage of your holdings in cash and/or invested in bonds (long-term bonds could be very risky when the interest rates is going up). Those wealthy enough can fully invest in stocks as losing 50% of their portfolio doesn't alter their lifestyle. Most business owners should invest in stocks and other vehicles instead of plowing back to their businesses in order to diversify their investments.

Portfolios with more than a billion dollars such as in most mutual funds owning 10 stocks with 100 million each are just too risky to me.

Holding cash is safe but it loses its value due to inflation. To illustrate this point, consider these three scenarios in 1950:

1. An apartment bought in for $10,000 in NYC or in your home town.

2. An investment in the Dow Jones 30 Industrials for $10,000.

3. A 3.5% certificate of deposit or one of the U.S. Treasuries for your $10,000.

By now, all real estate investments should have appreciated many, many times over and most stock shares value would have multiplied also. The $10,000 CD gain has lost real value due to inflation. Our capitalist system punishes us for not taking risk. In the long term, risk is smoothed out over time.

- Excessive frequency in re-balancing your portfolio for diversification takes up time from evaluating stocks. It may cost you in transaction fees but they are low in today's self-directed brokerage accounts. In addition, it may have some tax consequences in taxable accounts.

The advantage of churning the portfolio (but not excessively) can improve the quality of your portfolio with most updated information about the companies you invest in.

Many brokers display your current diversification in your monthly statement summaries. If not, use a simple spreadsheet to classify the sectors and the asset classes in your portfolio.

- Diversification can easily be achieved by buying indexed funds and/or ETFs. They are less volatile. I recommend it to all folks with less than $50,000 to invest.
- Diversification does not mean to pick simply a stock in other sectors that has the opposite correlation from the stocks you own. The stock quality comes first.
- Diversification takes a back seat to spotting market plunges. When most stocks plunge such as during 2007-2008, diversification does not save your portfolio, but spotting and reacting to market plunges will.
- Some of our stocks will lose value. If they were due to our mistakes, write them down and learn from them. If they were frauds (not avoidable in many cases), diversification would limit our losses
- Over diversified is not too good either. With too many stocks you own, you may not have time to monitor them. Focus investing could be very profitable.

My suggestions on diversification

Portfolio up to	Strategy	For stock pickers
$ 50,000	ETF that simulates the market	5 stocks
$100,000	80% in ETF and 20% in a sector ETF(s)	10 stocks
$500,000	10 stocks with less than 3 in same sector.	15 stocks with less than 3 in same sector.
$1 Million	15 stocks + at least 20% in ETFs.	20 or more stocks depending on your time available and less than 4 in same sector.

As described, everyone's situation is different. If you have more time for investing, you should be able to handle more than 10 stocks. Playing market timing (i.e. switching to cash) depends on one's risk tolerance. If you are good at stock picking, you should buy stocks instead of ETFs. On a personal note, I usually have more than 10 stocks.

11   Covered calls

For basic descriptions on a covered call from Wikipedia, click here or enter (http://en.wikipedia.org/wiki/Covered_call) in your browser.

It is like collecting rent from the apartment you bought. The difference is that the renter has an option to buy the apartment at a preset time and price.

The rent is quite substantial if you do good planning. To start with, you want to buy stocks that have a market to sell. Usually they are large companies with high trading volumes.

Since one contract is for 100 shares of a stock, you cannot sell a covered call on 50 shares of a stock. On the other hand, when you have 1,000 stocks, the commission of 10 contracts would be more than the cost of 1 contract depending on your broker's schedule.

It is time consuming to keep track of the covered calls but it is well worth your time and effort. If the stock price exceeds the strike price of your covered call, you may want to buy the same shares back, so you would not miss any further appreciation of this stock.

However, if it is in a taxable account and you have a loss in a forced sell, do not buy it back otherwise the tax loss is not allowed (i.e. a wash sale) for the year as of 2016. When the contract expires, you may want to start another contract on the same stock if the stock has   not   been   sold.

Covered calls do have their disadvantages such as higher commission rates and sometimes forcing you to sell at a higher tax rate for short-term capital gains in taxable accounts. It is avoidable by using covered calls on stocks that are qualified for long-term capital gains. In addition, you need to buy them back when they increase in price beyond your strike price or lose its potential to appreciate further. Using another put could keep you from not losing any gains beyond the strike price. However, I prefer to use my time in more productive ways and this insurance is not cheap. One's opinion.

One company advertises their techniques using covered calls which could give their users 3 to 6% monthly returns. If you believe in this fantasy, you do not need this book. There is no free lunch.

My recent experience

I sold Netflix covered calls with the strike price about 2% higher and a 3% premium (from my memory) but the price shot up 12% higher in one day, so I was potentially losing 7% profit. However, it turned out to be a good experience as Netflix went downhill later (8/2012).

Normally I prefer to sell covered options for stocks with a quantity from 100 to 600 shares (i.e. 1 to 6 contracts) for the longest time (about 2-3 months). Some non-volatile and small stocks are not candidates to write covered calls on. Some stocks are not optionable. Typically high-tech stocks have a higher premium to be collected as their stock prices fluctuate more. The right stocks can generate 10% or even more a year in addition to the fluctuations of the stock prices.

In general, if I feel the market will be down for the period, I use covered calls especially for stocks holding over one year (unless I have short-term loss to offset any short-term gains) in taxable accounts. Watch out for any tax change that may affect your total return.

Recently I attended a sales pitch on a 3-day training course on a strategy for making 24% per year and it is quite possible especially with the S&P 500 returns about the same. I wish it were available to me 15 years ago. It seems to be too good to be true.

How to sell covered calls

First you need to open an account with your broker and apply to trade options including covered calls.

Check how your broker charges commissions. Ask how much they charge for one contract and 10 contracts of a stock.

The covered call is an agreement to sell the rights to the buyer of the stock at the strike price for a specific date range (a.k.a. expiration date). Typically options expire on Fridays.

You need to write covered calls on the stocks you already own. One contract is 100 shares of stocks. Check out the option chain to select the price, expiration period and the strike price. Normally, the strike price should be higher than the current market price. You may want to have an expiration date 2 weeks or longer. When the contract is expiring in a few days, the contract has little value and most likely the small 'rent' is not worth the risk and the commission.

When the covered call is sold, you receive the 'rent' immediately and any dividend during the 'rental' period.

When the option is 'called' due to a price rise above the strike price, your stock will be sold and you will have to pay the regular commission.

At this point, evaluate the stock to check whether you want to buy it back. If the stock surges, you may have to pay a higher price – thus losing the extra appreciation. In addition, you may have to pay a higher capital gains tax if it is held less than the required period for long-term capital gains in a taxable account.

Note. Notice that some stocks are not optionable and/or not practical to write options on. Most brokers charge a flat rate for the first contract (such as $7) and an incremental fee for each additional contract. Shop around as the fees vary if you write a lot of covered calls.

The best stocks for covered calls are large US companies with a large average volume. The option (a.k.a. the 'rent') pays better for volatile companies such as high-tech companies. From my rough estimates for illustration purposes, the annualized return on covered calls for AAPL is 25% and C is 12% after commission.

#Filler: Double standard
We set up our standard in everything and the entire world has to follow our standard. Shooting citizens at each other, separating children from the illegals, and police brutality are fine according to our standard.

12   My A.B.C. on bonds

Bonds are classified into several categories and each has its different characteristics. Briefly, they are classified as 30-year Treasury bonds, 20-year Treasury bonds, 10-year Treasury bonds, short-term Treasury bonds, municipal bonds, investment-grade corporate bonds and high-yield (junk) bonds.

As of 5/2013, the long-term Treasury bonds are very risky. The interest rates is so low and it has no way to go but up. It will when the economy is improving. I do not expect we are following Japan's low interest rates for last decades.

Here are random comments on bonds.

- Japan has almost virtually zero interest rates for a long while. If you borrow 1 M from them at almost 0% and invest in another country's bond at 8%, you may think you win. However, you need to consider the risk in converting the country's currency back to Japanese Yen, inflation, bond loss, and taxes.

- In 2008, almost all assets lost. However, some high-yield bonds (or junk bonds) made over 40% in 2009. To illustrate, you bought these bonds yielding about 8% dividends in the beginning of the year. The government lowered the interest rates to stimulate the economy and hence the average yield was about 1% at the end of the year. The bonds you held yielding 8% were worth far more than the current bonds yielding 1% as they provide better dividends for years to come.

- As of 4/2012, the interest rates is almost too low to invest in bonds to me.

  Even the king of bonds made the wrong call. Do not bet against the Fed as they control the interest rate. They will raise the interest rates when they think the economy is ready.

  Conventional wisdom tells us to balance your portfolio with a combination of bonds and stocks in proportional to the risk tolerance, which for some is determined by their ages. I prefer the reward/risk ratio and only buy bonds when interest rates is expected to fall which usually occurs after the first six months of a market plunge. The government has to simulate the economy by lowering the interest rates in almost all recessions.

Repeating the important prediction, as of 4/2013, the long-term bond crash seems to be coming. When the economy improves, the interest rates will rise. The interest rates is so low now that it has no way to go but up. It will affect adversely to the bonds you're holding especially the ones with low interest rates and long maturity from today.

- The government bond prices could collapse when its issuing country is printing too much and depreciating its currency.

  A bond at 20% yield may not be good if the company/country has more than 25% chance to default on their bonds.

- Those holding the GM bonds before the reorganization (i.e. the first bankruptcy) lost more than 40% of the bond values. Corporate junk bonds (i.e. high yield bonds) have its risk. Buy a bond fund or ETF on corporate bonds.

- The muni bonds are risky to me. I do not really care about the small tax advantages. Many may default. If you still want to buy them, buy a bond fund to spread out the risk instead of buying individual muni bonds. Detroit bankruptcy is a good example of this. This article was published far earlier than the collapse of several towns in California and now Detroit.

- The long-term bond price moves in the opposite direction of the interest rate. It is about a 1 to 5 ratio by my rough estimate. If the interest rates moves 5% up, then the long-term bond price would move 25% down. It is very rough estimate as it also depends on how long will the bond matures.

- Few sell the bond until it matures. If you need a steady income, buy government bonds at an acceptable rate (for example, greater than 8%). 2012 is not a good year to buy bonds with the low interest rates. Some bonds did default and the owner lost most or even the entire investment. The GM bonds before its first bankruptcy is one of them though it is quite rare.

- China has been a big buyer to our US treasury bonds. China does not want to kill the goose that lays the golden eggs. They need a good economy in the USA in order to sell their stuffs, which would create jobs for its citizens.

Afterthoughts

- This article was originally written in 2012. If you followed the advice not to buy long-term bond, you will save a lot of money. The traditional allocating between bonds and stocks is wrong. The decision of buying long-term bonds should be based on the current interest rates and its direction.

- Bond ETFs: TLT (20+ years Treasury Bond).

  Contra Bond ETFs: TBF (Short of TLT). Click here for an article on contra Bond ETFs.
  http://seekingalpha.com/article/1305371-strategies-for-a-rising-rate-environment-inverse-bond-funds?v=1365862967&source=tracking_notify

  Click here for other bond and contra bond ETFs.
  http://seekingalpha.com/article/1305371-strategies-for-a-rising-rate-environment-inverse-bond-funds#comment_update_link

- To respond to my 'Edu-mercial' (my new term) in 5/29/13, JTS said, "Very educational. Thanks! I'll be out my bond funds end of the day."

- Using rising interest rates as an example, the long-term Treasury bonds with lower interest rates may not fare well than the newly-issued, long-term Treasury bonds with higher rate

- Many financial advisors are trained to sell bonds. Many split the investment into stocks and bonds according to the client's age. It makes sense to them and their clients. It does not make sense to me especially on long-term bonds which are interest sensitive.

Bonds do not have a better record than stocks. As in my chapter on Market Cycle, I advise to buy long-term bonds only when interest rates is high and / or the rate is going to plunge. Muni bonds have been advised to stay away more than a year ago and now we have Detroit, a major city, going to bankruptcy.

- Avani: This article is mind blowing. I read it and enjoyed. I always find this type of article to learn and gather knowledge.

- Buying a bond fund and an individual bond could be quite different. Bond funds usually buy a large number of bonds maturing in different periods. The mature periods are according to the objective of the fund such as long-term bond funds.

- There is a way to structure buying funds varying in maturity periods to lower the risk of the interest rates fluctuations. Check your broker to see whether they provide such a tool.

  However, I believe it could be better to buy long-term bonds when the interest rates is high (say 8%). A 3% yield does not beat inflation (which is about 3%) even without including taxes.

- Mortgage REIT is similar to long-term bond. Click here for an article.
  (http://seekingalpha.com/article/1548162-mortgage-reit-meltdown-i-told-you-so?v=1373916710&source=tracking_notify)

Links

Bonds:
http://en.wikipedia.org/wiki/Bond_%28finance%29

Fidelity:
Bonds vs. Bond Funds
https://www.fidelity.com/learning-center/mutual-funds/bond-vs-bond-funds

13   Tax avoidance

Tax avoidance is a good way to save some money legally. Tax laws change all the time. Check Wikipedia on current investment taxes. Consult your tax lawyer as my knowledge in taxes is limited, and the tax laws are always changing.

In general for Federal returns on your taxable accounts (as opposed to IRA, Roth IRA, IRA-Rollover and 401K), you have to pay taxes on dividends either at the ordinary income rate or at a qualified rate which is usually lower. If the stock that was held longer than a year, you pay long-term capital tax (max. 20%). The short-term capital tax rate at the ordinary income rate up to 37%. In addition, you may have to pay state and local taxes. Currently, you can offset $3,000 or up to your total losses from your regular income.

Do not implement what I did as tax laws change frequently and every one's situation is different. Here is what I did and I hope it will be applicable to you.

- Sold most profitable stocks that I held more than a year in taxable accounts in 2011 to qualify for long-term capital gains. Usually they have more favorable tax treatments than the short-term capital gains, which are treated as ordinary income. I bought some back. I maintained a 15% tax bracket, so the tax bill from Uncle Sam is virtually 0 (not exactly due to more tax on social security and Medicare as a result of the trades). I still had to pay state tax. As a retiree, I can control my income.

- Converted part of my Rollover IRA to Roth in 2012 and 2013. I paid taxes today. However, the Roth conversion gives me tax-free appreciation for the future trades in this account and it will lower taxes and my minimum withdrawal requirement in the future. Check whether it is still available.

- The taxes from dividends in the retirement accounts are deferred but eventually they will be treated as regular income when they are withdrawn. Very few people have higher income during their retirement. If you are the lucky few due to the successful investing in your retirement accounts, you may end up with a higher tax bracket during your retirement, particularly when you are forced to withdraw at age 70 ½.

- Gifted some appreciated stocks to my children. The current price of the gifted stock is used in calculating the total cost allowed, not the price you paid for them. I prefer the value stocks that have potential for long-term appreciation. It is good for them and not good for Uncle Sam. You can gift up to $15,000 (in 2019) for each spouse to each child without paying any Federal tax. For a family of four, you and your spouse can gift up to $60,000 (= 15,000 * 4) a year.

  The link: https://www.irs.gov/businesses/small-businesses-self-employed/frequently-asked-questions-on-gift-taxes

  The cost basis of the transferred stock is quite complicated. Check out the current tax law. The cost basis of the appreciated stocks are carried to the receiver, so it would lower your capital taxes as most of us are in higher tax brackets than our children.

  From my experience, the cost basis of the depreciated stocks after the transfer is the market price on the transfer day as of 2016. I do not understand it enough to comment but just to tell you what I have experienced. I tried to offset my son's unexpected short-term capital gain by transferring a losing stock and that does not work.

- My lawyer set up trusts for me including my house. They will avoid probate hopefully. From the current tax law (as of 2016), the cost basis of your stocks will be stepped up or down to the stock prices on that day you pass away. Ask your heirs to keep a business paper for the stock prices or tell your brokers to adjust the cost basis on the day you pass away. Of course, you have to tell your heirs now to take care of these tasks. Again, ask your tax lawyer for details.

  Make sure you specify the beneficiaries in your and your spouse's accounts to avoid probate. Check your local state laws. Some states take more than a year to finish the probate process for a house. As of 2014, my state (Mass.) has an exemption of 1 million, not portable to your spouse, and they calculate the entire estate when it exceeds the exemption. There is no estate tax if my estate is a million dollar. I have to pay a rate on 1,000,001 if it just exceeds it by one dollar. That's why we should move 30 miles north to New Hampshire.

I estimate that it takes about three years for the average estate to be distributed. You want to cut down the duration by having a will to start with, so you do not want to pay extra for your lawyer.

- At age 70 ½ (as of 2016), you are required to withdraw them in a schedule and it could put you in higher tax bracket. Roth withdrawal is not counted in the mandatory withdrawal for a person's lifetime as of 2016.

- Roth IRA if qualified could be the best deal for most. However, you have to use after-tax money to fund your Roth IRA.

- I simulate my next year via my tax preparation software and adjust my income accordingly.

- Most oil partnerships and many MLPs require you to file special tax forms for non-retirement accounts in 2017. I avoided most of them as my time is limited. Some ETFs require you to file the complicated K-1 (vs 1099) in your tax return. You can find this requirement in ETFdb.com. You can avoid them by not buying these ETFs; I prefer to buy them in my non-taxable accounts (i.e. retirement accounts). Usually the taxes on these dividends are lowered as they are treated the return of investment after depreciation.

- Avoid wash sales in your taxable accounts
  http://en.wikipedia.org/wiki/Wash_sale

You cannot claim the loss for the year if you buy back the stock within 30 days. Before I buy, I check whether I sold this loser in the last 30 days. Before I sell a loser, I check whether I bought it in the last 30 days.

I placed one order to sell a loser at a higher price and another one to buy it back at a lower price. When there is a big swing in price for that stock, both orders were executed within 30 days. I cannot claim the loss of the sold stock for that year. However, the loss can be adjusted to the cost basis of the newly-acquired stock as of 2013.

There are many ways to avoid it. Try not to buy it back within 30 days (check the current regulation) and this is the best way. IRS has more restrictions and it is better not to push it to the limit. Buy a similar stock in the same sector. Buy it in your children's account. Again, check the current tax laws.

Afterthoughts

- Tax audit signs.
  http://money.cnn.com/gallery/pf/taxes/2014/03/14/tax-audit/index.html?iid=HP_LN
  Your business would be treated as a hobby if you do not have a profit in three out of the last five years. Day traders and businesses can deduct all the trading expenses. Some form an investing company in some Caribbean island to avoid paying taxes. Again check the current tax laws.

- As of 2013, the dividend tax is at 20% max. Do not believe it is no tax in tax-deferred accounts. When you withdraw, it will be treated as a regular income and it can be as high as almost 40% (as of 2013). Your dividend tax rate depends on your income.

- When you trade 5 times or more a week, investigate whether you're eligible to trade as a business by the current tax rule. A business allows its owner to deduct business expenses.

- Fidelity: Investment tax.
  https://www.fidelity.com/learning-center/mutual-funds/tax-implications-bond-funds

  ETF Taxes on Foreign Stocks:
  http://seekingalpha.com/article/2491465-foreign-withholding-taxes-in-international-equity-etfs

Links
Tax Avoidance:
http://en.wikipedia.org/wiki/Tax_avoidance

14   Technical analysis (TA)

The basics

Technical analysis (a.k.a. charting) is easier to learn than you might expect. It represents the trend of the market (a stock or a group of stocks) graphically. If more investors are in the market, the market would move upwards until it changes direction. We divide the trends into short-term, intermediate-term and long-term.

The chartists usually do not consider fundamentals as they believe they have already been priced into the stock price and some fundamentals are not available to the public. To illustrate, a new drug has been discovered, the stock price of the company jumps initially by insiders purchases and the informed. Its fundamental metrics do not demonstrate this right away, but many investors are buying to boost up the stock price as evidenced by the technical indicators such as SMA for 20 or 50 days.

The volume is a confirmation. When the stock moves up or down by 10% with a low volume, the trend is not yet confirmed.

The trend of the stock price is not a straight line in most cases. Hence a trend line is usually drawn to indicate the direction of the stock. Many investors believe the stocks fluctuate in certain ranges (i.e. channels) and the chart draws the upper value (the resistance line) and the lower value (the support line). In theory, the price of a stock fluctuates within the resistance line (ceiling for understanding) and support (floor). When it reaches its support, it becomes a buy and vice versa for a sell. Most charts including Finviz.com would display these lines.

When the price passes out of the channel, it is called a breakout. Darvas, one of the oldest and most successful chartists, profited from the breakouts of the resistance line and believed the stock was close to the support line of the new channel. Hence it would be a long way up in theory.

If it were so simple, there will be no poor folks

It works most of the time, but do not place all your money on it. For chartists, 51% is great (the same for playing Black Jack). Some trends reverse very fast such as the bio drug stocks in 2015. You need to hedge your bets such as placing stop orders. Most do not want to spend their lives in watching the trend from a big screen.

Most novices use too many technical indicators and lose in their performances to the professionals. Recently, most chartists were not doing all that great and I did not find many books on their success than a decade ago. It could be due to too many followers in similar setups. I verified it with my recent testing using Finviz.com.

Simple Moving Average

The basic technical indicator is SMA-N. It is the average of the last N trade sessions. When N is 20 (or SMA-20), we classify it as short-term. Similarly, SMA-50 is an intermediate-term and SMA-200 is long-term. I prefer 50, 100 and 250. This trend duration is important. For example, do not want to place long-term purchases using the short-term SMA-50. There are many modifications to SMA such as giving more weight to recent data, but I have not found them any better. Finviz.com includes this information without charting (SMA-20, SMA-50 and SMA-100 in percentages).

Defining the trend periods is rather arbitrary. I use SMA-350 to detect the market plunges and SMA-100 for stocks. Weighted Moving Average weighs more weight on recent price data.

It can be used to determine whether we are in bull, bear or a sideways market using SMA-50 (or SMA-200 for longer term) for the market (using SPY), the sector (using an ETF for the sector and the specific stock. The trend is up when it the price is above the SMA and the reversal of the trend.

https://www.youtube.com/watch?v=jdYNaE5GJOk&list=WL&index=5&t=609s

The trend is your best friend
Most traders use TA for trending in a short duration. Investors can also use TA to time the entry and exit points for better potential profits. Value investors usually are patient and they do bottom fishing and they search for 'oversold' condition using RSI(14). Again high volume is a confirmation.

Many sites provide charting free of charge such as Yahoo!Finance. Finviz.com provides a lot of technical indicators without charting such as SMA% and RSI(14). It also provides screen searching for stocks that meet your technical analysis criteria.

Hands on

Bring up Finviz.com and enter any stock symbol such as AAPL. You can see the daily prices of AAPL from about nine months ago to today. Three SMAs (Simple Moving Average) are displayed as SMA-20, SMA-50 and SMA-200. The first two are for short-term trends. When the price is above the SMA, it is expected to be trending up. Again, the trade volume is used as a confirmation.

You can also see the resistance line and the support line drawn. In theory, the stock will trade within these lines. When it exceeds its resistance line, it is called a breakout, and vice versa for a breakdown. Sometimes it displays some technical patterns such as Cup and Shoulder and Double Down (both are positive patterns).

Select Weekly data. The Candle chart is better described than the Daily chart. Candles give us better descriptions of the price: open, close, high and low. The green color indicates the price is up for the period (a week in this example) and the red color indicates a down period.

In addition, Finviz.com includes some technical indicators in the metric section such as RSI. Most other chart sites are similar in the basics. Use Finviz's Help and select Technical Analysis for more description. Investopedia has enhanced descriptions on this topic.

TA patterns

There are many TA patterns such as Bollinger Bands and MACD. The patterns are based on the stock prices and many times they prove to be correct predictions especially on stocks with high volume and high market caps. Patterns have been repeating themselves many times as they are driven by investors.

Sites for TA

There are many free sites for charts with explanations of their technical indicators. Popular ones include BigCharts.com,

SmallCharts.com and Yahoo!Finance. Fidelity includes some unique features in its charts such as P/E.

Why I do not use TA as a primary tool for stock picking

My investing style is different from a day trader's. I prefer to 'Buy Low and Sell High' instead of 'Buy High and Sell Higher'. I try to find the real bottom price. TA will not find the bottom very easily but it tracks the trend better. As a bargain hunter, I do not expect the stock will rise fast as I'm usually swimming against the tide. However, value stocks could stay in the low price for a long time (i.e. value trap). I like to select stocks that turn around as evidenced by the SMA-20 and SMA-50.

With that said, my momentum portfolio has appreciated consistently and usually has the best performing stocks among all my portfolios. It is based on the timely grade from my subscriptions plus the metrics on timing.

Most chartists would also tell you to buy the stocks that have broken out (i.e. higher than the resistance line) and/or stocks at their highs. Contrary to value investing, you should exit when the trend reverses. The reversal could happen very fast and hence protect your portfolio by setting up stop loss (preferably with trailing stop) orders.

My opinion

I do not want to argue whether TA is good for you or not. You need to find that out. Most likely, the day traders and very short-term traders will profit more from TA than the investors seeking value stocks for the long-term gains.

Random remarks

Even if you do not use technical analysis, you should spend some time in learning it. It is better to marry fundamentals and TA. My random remarks are:

- The Institutional investors (insurance companies, pension funds, mutual funds, etc.) use TA and they MOVE the market. A lot of times it becomes a self-fulfilling prophecy. It is better to join them as most of us cannot beat them.

- Day traders take advantage of the institutional investors by spotting their trends.

- Most TA stocks should be good sized and have large average daily volumes. I prefer to use TA on value stocks to prevent long-term losses.

- I do know some folks making big money using TA, but I know more making good money using fundamentals. Since TA predicts the market better in the shorter term, its practitioners may have to pay higher taxes (in today's tax laws) in taxable accounts.

- Our objective should be making money with the least risk. Once you claim to belong to a certain group of either Fundamental or TA, you will be biased and forget your primary objective in investing.

- TA tracks the last two big market plunges (2000 and 2007) pretty well. The chart will not warn you right away for the upcoming plunge (as it depends on past data) to avoid the initial losses, but they will warn you to avoid bigger losses.

Afterthoughts

- Besides searching for stocks that have potential breakouts, we should check the stocks we owned for potential breakdowns. Technical Analysis tutorial.
https://www.YouTube.com/watch?v=GENBVwV8PMs

  SMA tutorial.
https://www.YouTube.com/watch?v=Na-ctpPsnks

Links

Fidelity video: Technical Analysis
https://www.fidelity.com/learning-center/technical-analysis/chart-types-video

Stage 4: Protect your wealth

1   Sector rotation in a nutshell

Introduction

I have been rotating sectors in my annuity for quite a long time and this strategy has increased my investment about four times over these years. My employer had a lot of restrictions for me in trading stocks, so switching to sector funds in my annuity was the best investment for me. When your account grows to a large amount, it is better to use a subscription service to help determine the rankings of your sectors.

For a starter, I recommend to paper trade your strategy. Use Seeking Alpha and/or Finviz.com to select the best performing sectors and/or use my quick analysis of ETFs. Switch it every month (or two) to the ETF corresponding to the best sector. Again, switch to cash when the market is riskier.

After a basic beginning, this book provides many features to help further refine your strategy. Use Technical Analysis. Start with the technical indicators such as SMA-50% and RSI(14) and a handful of sector ETFs to rotate (suggested sectors are technology, banking, health care, housing, consumer and material).

In addition, some sectors are more profitable in different phases of a market cycle. Here we examine several industry sectors and country sectors in more detail. The rise of China is affecting the global economy. When the interest rates is low, it would affect bonds and stocks yielding high dividends.

Many books ignore market timing. It turns out to be the most important profit maker from the last market plunges that have had an average loss of 45%!

The key to profitable sector rotation

Sector rotation could be very profitable and less risky than most of us would expect. There are two ways to profit:

1. Buy when the sector is trending up and sell when the sector is trending down. It is the common approach to sector rotation.

2. Buy at the bottom of a sector and sell at the peak. It is hard to detect the bottom/peak. It will be briefly described in the next part.

The following is a very basic way to rotate sectors. Many investment subscriptions and free sites such as Seeking Alpha and Finviz select favorable sectors every month. We assume the best-performing sector last month will perform better in the coming month. It does not always happen such as the tech sector in April, 2000 and the reversed direction of the drug sector in 2015. To protect your investment, use mental stops to avoid flash crashes.

Alternatively, we can select them via simple charts as described in this book. Beginners should start with Single Moving Average. Using more than one technical indicator without understanding them completely could cost you money.

Detecting the bottom of a sector
It is not easy and no one can detect the bottom or the peak of a sector consistently. The SMA-350 (Single Moving Average with 350 sessions) detects the market quite accurately for the last two market plunges. I have tested out the "days" with different numbers and 350 is the best fit for the last two market plunges.

Besides technical indicators, there are hints that indicate a sector is close to the bottom. Use the ETF for the sector and check out the fundamental metrics similar to evaluating a stock. To illustrate, enter XLE in Yahoo!Finance or Finviz.com to get the current price and other info about this sector.

Calculate the percentage of its current price from the bottom in the last 350 trade sessions. We assume the last bottom should be close to the next bottom in a sideways market. The intangibles should be considered too.

Detecting the trend
Detecting the trend is easier than detecting the bottom/peak. To illustrate, bring up Finviz.com from your browser and enter XLE. For most sectors, I use the SMA-50 (50-day single moving average), which is readily available as one of the metrics. When the stock price

is 3% above the SMA, buy it. When it is 3% below the SMA, sell it. It is that simple, but it has been proven many times.

You can adjust the 50-day and the 3% (some use 1%) to how long your average holding period of an ETF or a stock and then how often you want to trade. If your holding period is longer, use higher number such as 90 days. If you want to trade more often use 1% instead of 3%.

Personally I use 60 days if I use charts (from Yahoo!Finance among one of the many free sites that provide charts). One of my accounts requires 60 days for a minimum holding period without incurring a fee.

To detect market crashes and when to reenter the market or a sector ETF or a mutual fund after the crash, I use 350 days (some use 300 days). The 'days' is actually trade sessions.

RSI(14) indicates whether the sector is overbought or oversold. RSI oscillates between zero and 100. Traditionally, and according to Wilder (the author of the method), RSI is considered overbought with a value above 70 and oversold with a value below 30 as described in the article. This indicator is available from Finviz.com.

(http://stockcharts.com/school/doku.php?id=chart_school:tec hnical_indicators:relative_strength_index_rsi)

A simple way is to buy last month's winner(s). Ensure the ETFs are not leveraged if you are conservative. Aggressive investors can include contra ETFs when the market is risky. Here are the links to the websites that keep track of top performers varying 1 to 3 months.

Seeking Alpha's ETF Hub.
http://seekingalpha.com/insight/etf-hub/asset_class_performance/key_markets
Morning Star. Select the period (1 month for example).
http://news.morningstar.com/etf/Lists/ETFReturns.htm

What to buy
I prefer ETFs for specific sectors and sector funds (check out the holding period to exit without penalties) as another choice. Sector

funds are better than ETFs in specific sectors such as banking, drug companies and mining.

ETFs charge less for maintaining them and they have all of the advantages of a stock. However, mutual funds select the stocks within a sector selectively. Fidelity offers the most complete sector mutual funds. Compare the 3- or 5-year performance between the ETF and the sector fund in this same sector.

The third option is a top-down approach. First, when the market is not plunging, select the favorable sector and then the stocks within the sector. Many free sites provide a filter for favorable sectors.

Here is a list of sector ETFs.
(http://www.bloomberg.com/markets/etfs/)

Here is a list of commission-free ETFs from Fidelity.
(https://www.fidelity.com/etfs/ishares)

Some sector funds automatically switch sectors for you; however my experience did not prove to be profitable. Check out their past performance.

Favorable sectors according to the market cycle

Refer to the chapter on Market Timing and Spotting Market Plunges for specific strategies. I remind myself to close most positions when the market is plunging.

Favorable sectors according to the interest rate

It is similar to the above. Retailing, auto and housing are usually hurt by high interest rates. However, an improving economy would remove this disadvantage as more employed folks can afford big-ticket items.

Favorable sectors according to geography

This is not an easy task. China and India have had their best performing years. Japan had one of the best years in 2013 during the two decades. For foreign countries, currency fluctuation should be considered. Most emerging countries have their ups and downs.

Most ETFs or sector funds buy larger companies that are more trustworthy in their financial statements.

Global economies have never been that tightly connected to each other. When the US economy is down, China is affected and so are the resource-rich countries. Trump's trade war would have adverse effect on globalization that would lead to global depression.

Favorable and unfavorable events

The EU crisis has taken more than three years as of 4/2016 and the EU stocks are still close to the bottom. I prefer to buy an ETF specialized in EU or a mutual fund when the trend is up.

When the Treasury says the interest will be lower, the market and the long-term bond funds will move up, and vice versa. To me, the interest rates will move up slowly from the 1/2014 bottom. Most likely the new Fed chairwoman will not raise the interest rates until the economy totally recovers.

Recent favorable and unfavorable sectors

There are many sources available to check what sectors have performed more recently. Finviz.com is one of them. From the top menu bar, select Group, and the best and worst sectors will be displayed. Skip one day or one week unless you have a special interest in these short durations. Select the duration depending on your purpose. Personally I would use one month (or two) for my monthly rotation strategy betting the momentum would pass to the next month.

Technical analysis would spot the trend. Select a Simple Moving Average with n days. It is similar to the TA used in the chapter spotting market crash. Instead of using SPY or another ETF market index, use an ETF that represents the sector.

Sector rotation by fund managers

We cannot beat these institutional investors. We need to follow them or be one step ahead of them. They rotate sectors when they find another sector that has a better appreciation potential, or the current favorable sector has reached its peak.

When to rotate

Rotate for the following reasons:

1. When the market is plunging, rotate the sector ETFs and/or mutual funds to cash. Aggressive investors would rotate their equities to contra ETFs. The average loss of the last two market plunges is about 45%. This chart will not determine the peak as it depends on the falling data. However, it will tell you when to exit to prevent further loss and tell you when to reenter the market.

2. When the fundamentals of the current sector bought are turning bad.

3. When there is another sector that has a better appreciation potential. Finviz.com tells you the rankings of the sectors.

4. When the sector is overbought or peaking, and / or has met our objective.

Do not forget market timing
Do NOT buy any stocks except the contra ETFs when the market is plunging. Playing defensively usually wins the game more often than playing offensively. You can make good money without sector rotation by following market timing. When the market is peaking, protect your profits by placing stop loss orders.

Positions and how often to switch
It depends on the size of your portfolio and how much time you can afford to monitor your portfolio. To me, it varies from 2 to 6 positions and 20 to 90 days to monitor these switches.

Statistics show that a portfolio with 5 positions rotating in 20 days give you slightly better performance and less drawback (maximum loss for the period). I recommend 4 (2 for a portfolio of less than $20,000) and 30 days (and 60 days for Fidelity sector funds).

Conclusion
Sector rotation is described in very basic terms here. The links in Afterthoughts provide additional information. As a reminder, **roughly half of a stock's price movement can be attributed to the sector it is in.**

2   Dividend investing

This is a popular strategy now. It is expected to be so for the next 10 years or until the average CD rate beats the average dividend rate. We have a lot of retirees who depend on income from investments. The low interest rates from CDs and bonds drive these folks to dividend stocks.

Here is a simple screen to find these stocks. First find the stocks that have dividend rates more than 2% (about half of the S&P 500 stocks). Take out those sectors that give dividends as a return of equity (REITs and many partnerships). Eliminate the stocks with bad fundamentals such as high expected P/E, high debt (compared to companies in the same sector), etc. Next ensure that they have a good history of maintaining or increasing dividends (i.e. dividend growth).

As of 5-2014, it has been working well for the last five years. Follow my article on how to be cautious on bank stocks, the drug companies, the miners, the insurers and small foreign companies. In addition the stocks with good dividends fluctuate less in prices especially during market plunges.

However, when a strategy is over-used, it may not work any longer. There may be a mild bubble on these dividend stocks (due to too many followers). We will discuss how to protect our dividend portfolios.

In addition, we should not buy (actually should sell most stocks you own) stocks during a market plunge. I will describe how to detect market plunges and corrections. Since 2000, we have two market plunges with an average loss of over 45%. We hope to have a maximum loss of 25% and are ready to return to the market as indicated by the simple marketing technique described in this book. There are at least three variations on dividends:

1. Dividends given to stock owners (registered on and before the **ex-div date**).
2. Covered Calls. You can receive dividends while 'renting' your stocks.
3. DRIPs, Dividend Reinvest Plan.

The basics

Basic ratios for dividend stocks

- **Ex-dividend date**

You will be eligible for dividends if you have your stock on the record. You want to buy the stock earlier, or on ex-dividend date in order to receive the dividend.

- Payout Ratio

It is the dividend / profit. Too high a ratio may not be good as the company does not plow back the profit into research / development. Most mature companies have higher payout ratios as they do not need to plow back into research / development when compared to high tech companies.

The other option of using the company's cash is in a stock buyback that would increase the stock values in theory.

Earnings per share = Earnings / Outstanding Shares.

When 'Earnings' is fixed but Outstanding Shares are reduced, the ratio looks good deceptively.

- Dividend Yield.

It is dividend / price.

Why companies pay dividends

Companies can use the profit by plowing back cash into research / development, buying back its stocks, acquiring companies and/or giving dividends to the stock holders. In theory, the company should consider the option most beneficial to the average stock holder. In practice, the management tries to benefit them by choosing the option best to appreciate their stocks and hence they are granted stock options.

My additions to conventional dividend investing

Hopefully my additions would improve the performance of this strategy when it has already been proven to work.

- I add market timing to Dividend Investing. You need to sell most stocks before a market plunge and buy them back as indicated by the chart.

- Diversify your portfolio. Keep 10 stocks for a portfolio of less than a million dollars. Ensure not more than 3 stocks are in the same sector. Keep 20 stocks for portfolio over a million dollars. Holding too many stocks would require more of your time that would be better spent in evaluating individual stocks. Holding too few stocks would impact your portfolio when one stock has a big loss.

  It is just my recommendation. Vary your holding size and holding period according to your time frame, your portfolio size and your expertise in investing.

- Stick with stocks with a stock price over $2, an average daily volume of over 10,000 shares (8,000 for stock prices over $25) and a market cap over 200 million.

  Most big winners usually are in the price range of between $2 and $15 price and a market cap of between 200 million and 800 million. They represent the stocks that big boys are ignoring due to their restrictions. This is just a general guideline. Change them according to your requirements.

  I prefer to skip stocks from most emerging countries, especially the smaller companies as I do not trust their financial statements.

- Ignore the subscription services or books claiming that they make over 30% consistently. Some even have examples of making 5,000%. Most likely they will tell you about the winners but not their losers.

  Check whether their portfolio uses cash or not as they cannot short change in real portfolio. Most likely those portfolios that consistently make over 30% are not real. Ask for the proof of their account from a real stock broker and check the transactions.

Alternatively they have 10 portfolios and they may only show you the one that makes a good profit. They could use the most favorable trades for the day for their virtual account. For example, the stock rose 20% late in the day and they claimed that they bought it on the open hour. Hence, be careful not to fall for misinformation.

When they back test their strategies, they can cheat on their performances with survivor bias (i.e. those bankrupt stocks are not in the historical database). If their returns are that great, do you think they really will share their secrets with you?

Some made a big fortune and lost it all. So, the turtle investors who make small profits consistently and keep most of the wins fare far better than making millions in a year and losing it all the next year. Market timing and diversifying our portfolios help us win consistently in the long run.

Besides screening dividend stocks yourself, there are many sites providing this information. You can google 'dividend stocks'. The following are some of them.

TopYields
http://www.topyields.nl/Top-dividend-yields-of-Dividend-Aristocrats.php

An ETF on Dividend Aristocrats
http://etfdb.com/index/sp-high-yield-dividend-aristocrats-index/

From Wikipedia on the S&P Dividend Aristocrats
http://en.wikipedia.org/wiki/S&P_500_Dividend_Aristocrats

There are many sites to screen dividend stocks. I select Finviz.com as that should give us the best result and it is free. In addition, we use the same site for market timing.

Screening is only the first step. You need to filter the good stocks from the bad ones. When you have a handful of stocks, evaluate each one.

---

3   Newsletters and subscriptions

Why do you not see too many reviews on investment newsletters and subscriptions from the media? If it is a bad review, most likely they will not advertise in the media. If it is a good review, they may have to face legal actions in the future if the vendor's subscription or newsletter does not perform well.

I've been using investment newsletters / subscriptions for years. Many are priced reasonably and some are even free. While a lot of them are garbage, some are very good.

When you have a lot of money to invest and you're not using a financial adviser and/or not subscribing to any investment service, it could be a big financial mistake. You do not want to be a penny smart but a pound foolish. Very few have the knowledge and the time to make use of the free financial data, including the guidance and articles from the web.

You need a computer, access to the Internet and a spreadsheet in order to use most subscription services effectively.

I'm not going to compare specific services / newsletters at the risk of being sued, but I will include general pointers on how to select them. Yesterday's garbage could be a gold mine today if the subscription improves and/or the market conditions fit what they recommend.

First, you need to find out your requirements and how much time you can afford to use them. If you have $20,000 or less to invest, most likely your investment both in time and money will not pay off. Just buy an ETF and practice market timing described in this book. My pointers are:

- Newsletters giving you specific stocks to buy do not require much of your time. However, if they're successful, there will be too many followers buying the recommended stocks that can drive up the prices at least temporarily. The owner of the subscription service and his insiders will buy the recommended stocks before you unless they're not allowed to do so (who's enforcing this?). I had several of these newsletters, and so far I have not renewed any one of them due to the poor performance.

- If I found the Holy Grail of investing, do you believe I would share it with you for $100 or so? I only will after I invested my money first. My subscribers would push up the prices for me and then I could unload them before my subscribers.

  As an experiment, I am publishing a book every month with the title "Best Stocks, As of MM/01/YYYY" recommending a handful of stocks. Due to my relatively small positions and few buyers of the book, it will not have the adverse effects described. If it reaches a wide audience, I will not trade the stocks I recommended in my books. Most of my recommendations should be value stocks for long term hold unless the market is risky such as in 8/2019. My books will not be the Holy Grail as my aim is beating the S&P 500 Index.

- If the volume of the recommended stocks are small, they can be manipulated easily either by the newsletter owners and/or by your peer subscribers. The first ones to sell the recommended stocks win and the last ones to sell them lose.

- I prefer systems that can find a lot of stocks by providing many searches (same as screens). However, it will take a lot of time to learn and test their performance which can be obtained easily with a historical database. Most likely, you need to further research each stock screened. The screens would select a limited number of stocks for further analysis, so it will save you time for sure.

  From my experience, the best performance comes from the stocks that have been screened by more than one search especially for the short term (less than 6 months). My theory is that they've been identified for many folks and hence their prices could be jacked up. It is more profitable to buy them ahead of the herd and sell them before the herd. In any case, research the stock you are interested in.

- I have received promotional mail that indicates their incredible performances such as tripling the money. Just ignore them. If it is that good, most likely they will keep them for themselves. It is the same for seminars that boost some penny stocks. Most likely the recommended stocks would rise initially to lure you and other suckers to move it. Watch out! As of 2016, I do not see these junk mail as often as before; the public is smarter. They must have switched their promotions to YouTube.

- A 'guru' told me that he made a big fortune in silver a month ago. Guess what? He also recommended selling it two months earlier and lost a lot of money in doing so. He is always right but he will not advertise the times he was wrong. We call it a double talk technique.

- There are free trial offers (or deeply discounted) for most subscription services. Take advantage of them. Some services require you to spend a lot of time, so ensure you have the time. Keep track of the performance yourself via paper trading. Do not trust their 'official' performance.

- Subscribe to a newsletter that fits your style of investing. If you're a day trader, newsletters on long-term investing are not good for you. Some subscriptions handle all kinds of investing styles and you need to find the strategies and recommendations to fit your style. A short-term swing trade has different metrics than a long-term investor.

- Newsletters on penny stocks are risky for most of us. They may show you a list of big winners but they do not show you their losers.

  I define penny stocks as less than $2 (officially $5) and a market cap less than 100 M. However, I do buy stocks with prices around $2 or a capital cap less than 100 M. Actually I bought ALU at $1 but ALU's market cap then was about 2 billion at the time. The stocks with prices between $1 and $10 represent the most volatile stocks and a few are real gems. They are routinely ignored by most analysts.

- There are many sectors like drugs, mines, insurance and banks that retail investors cannot evaluate effectively. It is better to seek expert advice from specific newsletters. Check out their past performance and take advantage of the free trial offers.

- Remember there is no free lunch in life. The higher potential return of a stock, the riskier the stock is. To me, all trades are educated guesses. The more educated the guesses are, the higher chance they will perform in the long run. However, noting is 100% sure.

- Some newsletters / subscriptions save us time by summarizing the financial data by providing a value rank and a growth rank. Some provide a timely rank from the momentum of the price. When the market favors growth, you use the growth rank, and vice versa.

- Be careful with the information from radio and TV commercials. Many try to sell to peoples' fear and greed by overstating without necessarily telling the whole story. It is not possible to make 50% in covered calls consistently or making another gold rush from $400 to $1,800. One advertises the market will lose 80% in 2016. It is possible but not likely. [Update: The market was profitable in 2016.] They are tactics to get you subscribe to their services.

- TV financial shows usually exaggerate in order to sell their products. Analyze them before you act on the news.

- As retail investors, most of us cannot afford to do extensive research. Many researches and market opinions are available on the internet free. Start to search for such information from your broker's site and financial sites such as SeekingAlpha.com, MarketWatch.com, CNNfn.com and Yahoo!Finance.com. Analyze the news and some could be obsolete or could be manipulated with a hidden agenda by the time you get it.

- Do not trust the performance of newsletter providers. There are many ways to manipulate their performance.

- Most compare their performances with the S&P 500 index. It is legal for investment newsletters to inflate their performance with dividends while comparing to an index without including dividends.

  To illustrate, S&P 500 has an average annual return of 1% on appreciation and 1.5% on dividends for a total return of 2.5%.

Hence, the performance of a newsletter should compare itself to 2.5% not 1%.

- The performance of the last 10 years (I prefer last 5 years) is more important than that of 25 years. The last 10 years is a better prediction of the newsletter than the last 25 years as the weatherman has found out.

  More than one time, I have found a popular subscription that did not beat S&P 500 in the last 5 years but it did in the last 20 years. It could be that too many folks are using the same strategy.

- When the new major researcher takes over the subscription, s/he may not have the same expertise as the previous researcher.

- Ensure the subscriptions change their strategies according to the current market conditions. For example, 10 years ago ADRs (U.S. listed stocks of foreign countries) performed far better than today. The trend may reverse in the future.

- Few if any use real money for their portfolios, as they cannot cheat with real money. That's why you never achieve the compatible performance by following what the portfolio trades. Some can manipulate by using the best prices of the day. Some omit their losers. Do not trust any performance claims even from reputable monitor services unless the portfolios can be verified with real money.

  Some sample portfolios trade excessively and they may not fit your investment strategy in addition to excessive commissions and taxes.

- When a subscription service has several strategies (say 10 for illustration purposes), they will advertise the strategies with the best returns for a specific time period.

- Today (12/8/2014) TNH was down by 12% by the end of the day. If they used the open price, it would have made a difference of 12%

Making full use of a subscription

Most subscription services including the free (as of this writing) Blue Chip Growth have four grades for each stock: Value, Growth, Timely and a combination of the three. Some have only two grades: Value and Growth.

When the market is favorable to value investing, select the grade Value such as in Early Recovery, a phase in the market cycle defined by me. To emphasize one grade over another, divide it by the opposing grade such as Value/Timely if it can be done (a letter grade can be converted to a number).

IBD

Il use the composite grade of this popular service especially for day traders and short-term swing traders. It is more a momentum grade, but they do have a value grade. I evaluate their IBD50 stocks. Check out the recent performance of IBD50 as provided. It could be useful to have a second opinion of these stocks with another service.

Screen Basic under Screen Center. It lists the stocks with top IBD's metrics.

Leading sector under Screen Center. Basically it is the second and the third step of my Top-Down Investing strategy (the first step is market timing).

Next to the screened stock, click on the Stock-Checkup for a complete evaluation of the stock according to IBD.

GuruFocus

It is free to me as an author. I use the screener to find stocks in my book Best Stocks. I found there are a lot of useful features I had not used. It will be a perfect system if they provide a historical database for testing the screens.

The idea is following the institutional investors who drive the market. Besides this great concept, it offers many tools for analyzing stocks. It has a score system that has been proven. The following metrics are harder to find in other sites: F-Score, EV/EBIT, Shiller PE,

DCF... Many metrics are compared to its industry and its history. They are displayed in an easy-to-read graphics.

Insider trade and institution ownership are great features.

Fidelity

Fidelity is my primary broker. If your broker does not have similar features, deposit the minimum cash so you can access Fidelity's extensive research. I am not paid by them.

They have a learning center especially great for beginners. View Point under News & Insight has the outlook of the markets.

Afterthoughts

- My friend told me he saw an ad that would show him how to make $500 a day for working a few minutes before the market opens. He is nice enough to share his 'discovery' with me. If it is as advertised, I would be the first one to sign up. If it really works, it will not work very soon. When a strategy is over-used, it will not work. Unfortunately, a fool is born every minute as the same ad had been here for a while.

- Currently I spend about $1,500 for all subscription services. I believe $200-$600 should cover the basic. To start, you can use your broker's website for tools. Some have a lot of research for evaluating stocks and some even include searches. Try the biggest broker's research as they spend more on this area. Even if you do not trade with them, use their research by opening an account with the minimum balance.

- If the offer is too good to be true (like making $500 every day with little effort and little investing money), probably it is not. If they give you a free 50" TV for spending $299, most likely it is a trap with bait. Again, remember there is no free lunch.

  However, some baits are good like the free 30-day trial offer for an investment service or the free dinners I attended seminars on estate planning. It is part of the business cost. If I do not attend more than two dinners, eventually I would end up paying two free dinners for someone I do not even know. This book could be the best deal for your entire investment life if you invest time to read it, digest it and use the ideas that are applicable to you and the current market.

- Do not trust their claims and the past performance may not have anything to do with the current or future performance unless they are from reliable sources.

To illustrate how to monitor their recent performance, if they give you 20 stocks every week, save the prices and check their performance in the same period you usually hold the stocks. It has busted many well-advertised and very popular subscription services. I prefer to compare the performance to the S&P 500 index. It is better to compare it both in an up market and a down market as some strategies amplify their performances by selecting riskier stocks.

- On 5/2013, I received an ad boasting how great its portfolio performs from a well-known subscription on investing. The cumulative return from 2001 to today is an impressive 308% beating S&P 500's 43%. However, if you analyze it further, most of the big gains are made before 2009.

To prove it, I used their data and input their returns from 2009 to today. Their accumulative return is 37% while S&P 500 is 66%. Current data has better predicative power than the older data.

The moral of the story:

1. Read any claim with skepticism. Test it yourself.
2. The recent performance has better predictive power than the older data.
3. When a strategy is over-used, it will become less effective.
4. The market conditions change from time to time. Some strategies work better than others in different conditions and different phases of the market cycle.
5. Most likely their return includes dividends while the S&P 500 index does not.

4   Hedge fund 101

LTCM (a hedge fund named Long Term Capital Management), with two Nobel-prize winners, an excellent support team and the best technologies then, ran their hedge funds into the ground. Many hedge funds are closed due to fraud, and/or poor performance.

The primary purpose is supposed to 'hedge' your investments from market plunges / dips. Since 2008, the government has printed so much money, and it make the market recover and make the hedges (shorts, derivatives, etc.) unnecessary. In reality, most hedge funds today do not hedge.

Hedge funds get tons of press coverage as a Holy Grail type of investing. The media needs the advertising from this $2.5 trillion industry. It is similar to mutual funds but they take more risk for supposedly better returns. Most require higher minimum investments and more restrictions such as requiring longer periods before you can withdraw your money.

It could be the worst deal to most of their customers: 2% average up front and 20% average on your profit. It is more acceptable to me if the 20% is on profit over S&P 500's return. Why should I pay you 20% on my 10% profit when the market rises by 15%? In this case, my fund loses 5% relative to the market.

Well, if they consistently make a lot of money for you, maybe it is not too much to object to. However, most risk your money by betting big recklessly. When they win, they get 20% of your profit and they use you for advertising to lure in other suckers. When they lose *your* money, they do not lose a penny. It encourages them to take big risks. I do not know any hedge fund (HF) manager who pays you back for your losses.

An average mutual fund charges about 1.5% in management fees. An average hedge fund charges 2% so that would cover the expenses to run their office, market the products and for research expenses. The real compensation of an average hedge fund depends on the average 20% of the profit.

You would have better return by investing in a no-load index fund, or a diversified ETF than an average hedge fund. To calculate the average hedge fund performance, you need to include the many hedge funds that are out of business. To illustrate my pint, check out the performance of SPY in the last five years and that of the average hedge fund. However, SPY and similar ETFs are risky due to the heavy weighing on winners such as FAANGs.

After a hedge fund has failed, most fund managers just open another hedge fund (if they do not go to jail first due to fraud) and give you all the excuse for losing your hard-earned money. Some lose their reputation but you need to check them out well before you hire another one.

In 2011, the hedge fund industry did not beat the S&P 500 index fund after their fees. I bet the hedge fund industry will not beat the market after 2011.

Some hedge fund managers learn modern portfolio theories from Ivy League universities and apply them in the hedge funds. Often their theories are based on wrong testing procedures, or they cannot be sustained in real life.

Many invest in new companies and small companies where they would have big profit swings. They need to learn the business of the company in which they plan to buy the stocks, interview the owners, read between the lines, and double check whether the owners are telling the truth by talking to their competitors, vendors and customers. It explains the high cost for their research. We just need to look at the transactions of the insiders and/or use a low-cost subscription to find similar type of research. There is no need to travel to visit the company unless you want to.

Some use their specialties in certain sectors and that's fine. If they use derivatives, be careful and that's what resulted in our 2007 financial crisis. Derivatives could reduce the risk of the portfolio if they are properly used. If you still want to invest in them, ask for their methods and their historical performance. Very few hedge funds are good. When you find a good hedge fund, most likely it has been closed to new investors or its fees are outrageous.

The owner of a famous baseball franchise lost big money from a hedge fund that concentrated in the oil sector. Almost every ETF in this sector made good money that year, but he still stayed with the hedge fund and had similar miserable returns the following year. I did not blame him for his first mistake, but on his sticking with the same hedge fund after a losing year. It could be that the hedge fund gave him a hard time when he wanted to take his money out or he could be busy in his baseball franchise.

One hedge fund has a performance of 25% every year over a long period of time. The SEC, takes notes and then investigates whether they were using insiders' information. There are very few hedge funds with consistent performance beating the market after their hefty fees. If you find some, stay with them forever. One hedge fund was rated as the top fund and the next year it was out of business due to poor performance. Hedge fund managers chase after short-term returns as the outflow will be serious if they do not perform well. When they were successful recently, they had a hard time to perform with an excessive inflow of money. Both cost underperformance in the fund.

In 1980, this industry started with really capable fund managers and made good money for their clients. After that, every analyst wanted to open a hedge fund and most did not even beat the market after their fees. Alternatively, just buy the ETF SPY and relax, instead of waiting for the hedge fund to wipe out your savings. You need to know that this industry is not properly regulated.

Do not believe in any articles / ads praising how great the hedge funds are without knowing their credibility and any hidden agendas. The hedge fund indexes usually ignore the survivor bias of the bankrupted hedge funds and the early exits of many hedge funds.

Since the hedge funds very seldom keep the stocks more than a year, their capital gains would be short-term and hence would be taxed at a higher rate than the long-term capital gains. In addition, most funds have a 1–3-year lock-up period and only allow withdrawals on the first day of each fiscal quarter.

Update as of 1/2016

Hedge funds have not been doing very good since 2009 as there is nothing to hedge in a rising market. Only a very few are doing great. Learn what and why they are doing great. The reasons are obvious by now. The successful ones unloaded energy stocks and

Chinese stocks after the crisis but before the big losses. Some correctly shorted the sectors afterwards.

However, I still advise you not to buy hedge funds for the average investor:

- The better ones are not open to new investors or ask for a king's ransom.
- On the average (including the closed hedge funds), they're not doing very well after the high fees they charge.
- Even the good one last year could be a bust this year as they're betting high. Examples abound.

To make money, you need to depend on yourself. To start, play simple market timing. Buy value stocks when the market is not risky. Be patient. Evaluate your owned stocks every six months (I prefer 3 months if time allows) and then act accordingly.

Following these simple 'techniques' (or common sense), you should at least beat the market (or SPY) in the long run. It has been proven and being practiced by many successful retail investors among us.

Afterthoughts

- From WSJ, from 1999-2008, the hedge fund industry beats S&P 500 by 13% a year. From WSJ, from 2009 thru July 2012, it lagged the market by almost 8%.

  In 2011, the average hedge fund lost money when S&P 500 was flat. In 2012, the average hedge fund earned about 6% when S&P 500 was up 13%. It is 'genius' to buy an ETF representing the entire market instead of an average hedge fund.

- Now hedge funds can advertise.
  A pig wearing lipstick is still a pig. If you run 5 hedge funds, you will advertise your best fund. Advertising industry will benefit and eventually their investors if hedge funds will pay for this expense.

  http://finance.fortune.cnn.com/2013/07/10/sec-votes-to-let-hedge-funds-advertise/?iid=HP_River

- A hedge fund article from SA.
  http://seekingalpha.com/article/584861-hedge-funds-are-they-just-smooth-operators?source=kizur

- Another hedge fund fraud.
  http://money.cnn.com/2013/07/25/investing/sac-capital-charges/index.html?iid=HP_LN

- Gold even managed by a great hedge fund manager is down as of 7/2013.
  http://www.cnbc.com/id/100855708

- A famous hedge fund manager (so is the one on Sears) has big losses in JCP and shorting another company. It teaches us to diversify and be conservative.
  http://money.cnn.com/2013/08/26/investing/bill-ackman-sells-jcpenney/index.html?iid=HP_River

- In 50 years, the $10,000 investment will grow to $1,170,000 assuming a 10% return a year. However, about $700,000 will be the cost of the typical mutual fund. It will be better to buy an ETF (a far lower fee) and avoid market plunges described in my book.

- Hedge funds must have had a hard time in 2013. Hedging against a rising market is a fool's game. Another article to review.

Links

LTCM:https://en.wikipedia.org/wiki/LongTerm_Capital_Management
Hedge Fund: http://en.wikipedia.org/wiki/Hedge_fund

5   Advantages of a retail investor

How can we, the retail investors, beat the professional fund managers? It is not likely if you consider all those research resources they have. However, in reality, the average retail investor does not beat the market due to switching between stocks and cash at the wrong time. Via the greed, they invest at the peak of the market and via fears they divest at the bottom. They do not expect the market to return from the bottom but it always does.

Most fund managers are smarter than I, better educated in investing than I, have ten times more research tools than I and have ten times more computer power than I. However, most of them do not beat me, the average casual retail investor. In addition, I spend less time in stock research than an average fund manager (most are working at least 60 hours a week) - I have a life too and maybe they don't.

It could be:

- They cannot beat the market all the time. When they do, money flows. It is very hard for them to perform with extraordinary cash. When the market is depressing, everyone cashes out their funds. They need to sell stocks even though they may have better potential to appreciate.

  The saying "When there is blood in the streets, most likely it is the best time to buy" is correct. 2009 is a recent example. Fund managers cannot take advantage of this opportunity as most clients had cashed out.

- Most cannot play market timing freely and they have to satisfy all the rules set up for the fund. Every time they want to buy a stock, they need to ensure no rules have been broken such as a restricted percent of a stock to the fund. Most funds prohibit their managers from shorting, buy contra ETFs and/or maintain high cash positions. Basically, most are not allowed to react to the market when it is going up or down.

- When they trade, their high volumes are tracked by day traders who can ride on their wagons. Hence they have to pay more to buy and get less to sell.

- By my rough estimate, they have about 1,000 stocks (about 600 for larger funds) to deal with. I as a retail investor have about 3,000 stocks even skipping most stocks with prices below $2 or not listed in the three major exchanges.

  Their stocks have been fully evaluated by analysts and newsletters / subscriptions such as Value Line and /or some firms specializing in stock research for them. Hence, they do not gain any advantage by following their peers.

  The small and mid-cap stocks are risky but are more rewarding statistically. Many fund managers cannot buy them due to the size of their funds.

- Their performance as a group is actually worse due to the closing down of non-performing funds.

- Not nimble enough.
  By the time they have done all the research and received the approval to buy a specific stock, I may have bought the stock already. Usually it takes at least a week for a large fund to complete trading a specific stock.

- The high expenses.
  The fee is about 1.5% for the average fund. The expenses are 2% plus 20% on the profit for an average hedge fund. When the fund and the broker belong to the same company, watch out for how it can make its brokerage arm more profitable by jacking up the commission. The hedge fund's usual 20% of the profit and no penalty of losing your money encourage its fund managers to take bigger risks.

- Not spending enough time to do their own research.
  Most do not spend enough time on basic research and select the right strategies in current market conditions. They spend a lot of time in following the fund's and the company's objectives, rules and regulations.

- Wrong objective.
  The objective of most funds is beating the common index after expenses. Most fund managers do not want to take too much risk and their personal objective is job security. One will not lose the job if his performance is similar to a target index.

- o The reason for some of their good performance is due to taking too much unnecessary risk and the high leverage. Their performance improves when the market is good, but degrades when the market is down. When I see the market is coming down, I would park more cash and I only use leverage when the market is going up.

- o They buy the same stocks as their peers are buying. If they do not perform within a certain range of a benchmark, they get canned. Hence, they stay away from risky stocks that usually have better profit potentials. We pay them to research these risky stocks to separate the gems from the garbage, not to follow the herd of their peers.

- Retail investors have a lot of advantages over fund managers. However, I advise you not be day traders as beginners. Statistically most amateur traders lose money as they cannot compete with experienced, disciplined traders. My books do not teach you how to be a short-term trader. Even if you study several good books by great traders, most likely you will still lose money initially. No books can replace the actual trading experience.

  However, discipline, knowledge and due diligence will make you money in the long term as a turtle investor.

Filler: Gamma rays

Gamma rays are the most effective tool for weight loss. If you die because of the gamma rays, you will lose weight gradually, naturally and surely

Filler: Victims?

We're victims of our own success: A higher living standard means higher wages, more protections for our workers and more regulations for our environment. All these will make us less competitive.

6 Invest responsibly

We work hard, save money and invest. Our investing in stocks serves two primary purposes:

1. Good return on our money (as in any investment), and

2. Provide jobs and taxes for the government. However, in reality, the stock market is being changed to a big casino.

Companies need our investing money to develop new products and hire employees. When the company makes money, it supposedly pays taxes and in theory hires more employees. We would not have Apple paying taxes and hiring thousands of employees if we did not finance it initially via IPO. However, global companies can hire anyone in any country at the least costs (labor cost, regulation cost...).

This is the ideal purpose for investing. Investors choose the companies that produce the proper products and / or services mix that would be profitable and at the same time are good for society and the world. Apple is a good example.

We ought to pick companies that promulgate the society. Here are some evil industries:

- Tobacco companies.
  Do you invest in products that kill? Even if you do not smoke, the second-hand smoke (and even the third-hand smoke for unborn babies) still kills. We discourage smoking in U.S.A., while our tobacco companies are making great profits in Russia and China. The recent legalizing of an illegal drug will bring more deformed babies.

- Defense (offense is more appropriate) companies.
  Why do we need a carrier generated by two nuclear generators? We already have weapons to destroy the entire world by pressing a button. Boeing is partially OK with a small division in offense.

After shooting in Newtown, most stocks in gun manufacturing companies went down in prices (profits went up initially due to fear of the ban). Their P/Es based on past earnings will be exceedingly low. This is another example that P/E does not tell the outlook of the industry.

Unfortunately they are legal products. Special interest groups control our politicians like puppets. However, the children in Newtown will not die for nothing and even politicians cannot cover their eyes and conscience any more.

[Norman, my good friend, has a counter opinion:
Disagree with your premise on military companies. The United States has made a lot of money by upholding capitalism around the world. If we had no military, we could not protect our property rights here and abroad. Chamberlin proved that a weak country has no rights when the fascists come knocking.]

- Casinos, wine, fast food, soda...
  These are border line cases. They provide good services and products, if you do not take it to the extreme. They only hurt you but not others (except from drunk drivers).

Money is not everything in life once we have the basics. We should invest wisely and responsibly in products that will not harm us.

What's good if you made millions in a tobacco company that kills you via the second-hand smoke? How about the young kids killed every day by guns? It is sad but it happens every day.

Stop counting money with hands dripping in blood.

___

Afterthoughts

I had a tough time in arguing with a doctor. He cared about the dividends from his tobacco stock more than your health. I wonder whether money was his original motive to choose this noble profession. CVS has done a good deed by not selling tobacco products.

The legalized drug kills!

7   Are investors parasites?

First most of our initial investment money is from our hard-earned money during our work life unless you're lucky having money via inheritance or marriage.

The retired rich could live a decent life with the money accumulated without investing in the risky market. However, we invest for better return for ourselves, work our own way (vs. paying mutual fund managers to do the same), and take some risk ourselves.

We do not think we're the parasites to the society. Our investments have helped many businesses grow. In turn, these businesses pay taxes and hire workers who again in turn pay taxes. We, the investors, also pay taxes too on our profits from selling our winners, sales taxes and estate taxes when we pass away. The society should benefit   a   lot   from   our   investment.

If we live to 70s or 80s, we will still be physically able to work on our investments, but most laborers can't. Hence, we will contribute to the society longer as a group.

We also reward companies with good management and/or profitable products and punish companies with poor management and/or unprofitable products.

Buying future options helps the farmers to have insurance for crops the plant and/or tells them whether the crops will be profitable when they're harvested.

It is unfair for the hard-working, rich folks less chance going to heaven than the lazy, welfare recipients. The majority of the free loaders (also known as the able welfare recipients and cheaters) are the parasites but not the hard-working investors. The gate keeper of heave, please take notes.

It is politically correct to help the poor and punish the rich (via excessive taxes). When we tax the rich excessively and unfairly, the rich will give up the citizenship and move to countries where there are fewer punishments for hard works and taking risk. It could be the last straw that breaks the camel's back. We are experiencing the greatest exodus for the rich in the last few years. Many countries welcome our rich with incentives and open arms.

We treat the middle class unfairly. I invest my hard-earned money, pay taxes on my profits. When the rich are gone, we would be the group supporting the government and the poor. We paid for our entitlements such as the social security, so we cannot move to another country easier than the rich.

I do not object to help the poor, but should the middle class be taken care of first? I do object giving our taxes to the rich bankers for bringing down the economy when some should go to jail. Margaret Thatcher once said, "Socialism is destroyed by giving to the poor until we have nothing left to give". When the host dies, the parasites will die too.

Can anyone explain the following?

- The poor get 100% free health care (say in Mass.), while the middle class like me are very careful to decide whether to see a doctor or not. I have to pay a lot even after the insurance.

- The poor can go to nursing home free of charge and we only go when we have no choice as it is very expensive.

- Last time a lady in front of me in a super market with a real Gucci bag bought the best cut of steak with her food stamp card. She may be driving a BMW too. Welfare cheating is too common and too easy.

One common comment to me is: "Tony, you can spend all your money and be poor." Is he stupid or am I stupid? Or, our society encourages folks to be poor, lazy, dependent and stupid.

I do believe in fair taxing and redistributing our wealth. The able welfare recipients should be 'forced' to work, but should not take away the welfare benefits for taking a job. Welfare frauds should be punished. Clinton's work initial is good but it also has more holes than the Swiss cheese.

I belong to the middle class, which is being squeezed by those who do not pay Federal taxes and the top rich 5%. The top 5% are the geese that lay the golden eggs and can fly away to places where taxes are lowered and we can't.

Afterthoughts

- Norman's counter point.

Tony--You have come upon the current structural change in the global society. I don't agree with how you have addressed it, almost a racial slur on the lower working class. In many people's eyes, the capitalists are the parasites on society and they don't pay taxes, but hide the money in Ireland and Switzerland. When this depression is over, there will be a better distribution of wealth or the elite will suffer the same fate that Marie Antoinette did. In my opinion, there will have to be redistribution of wealth in order to maintain the demand for goods and services. 99% of this country is poor!

Tony: More than 40% of us do not pay Federal income tax. Representation without taxation is worse than taxation without representation. Guilty as charged? You decide.

- Why I love investing.

I learn most disciplines in investing via common sense. Even if you have a Ph.D. from a prestigious college or how tall and handsome you're, your accomplishment in investing is only measured by the performance of your portfolio.

I spend about two days a week now (after all those testing and readings in the last 10 years) in investing. That's why I can spend so much time in forums, write books and enjoy life too (yes I do have a life to your surprise). I can afford to make a mistake once a while and no one dies because of my error. Everything I learn now can be useful for the rest of my life. I work in any place I want and any time I want.

I'm my own boss. There is no one to report to me and I have no one to report to. There is no company politics. No one discriminates against my yellow face. I do not care about others' feelings when I trade except my own when I lose.

I can play offense and defense without asking for permission. I do not have to follow any regulation, any dress codes, any work hours... My commute is from my bed to the couch.

I would like to share my experiences in this book. For one who never writes more than three pages in my entire career and in a foreign language (I bet my English is better than your Chinese), it takes me to a new challenge. The main reason I wrote this book is I cannot find one that would benefit the retail investor from actual experiences.

From my profitable investment, I can afford to take an early retirement and concentrate my effort to find new and profitable strategies in stocks investing (my hobby now). Today and for my frugal living, I do not have to bet big to accumulate more money but to protect them. There are many 'great' investors died almost bankrupted. We do not want to follow their footsteps. Be conservative!

This is my payback to the society besides my taxes as I do not expect make money from selling books.

###

I've written several books on investing. It is fun to comment in financial sites. It helps me to kill time (especially when the market is too risky to invest) and learn from others. In marketing my books, I made a lot of enemies. For me, it is not worth it as my objective is helping my fellow retail investors and contributing to the investing world not to upsetting anyone. Today, Amazon.com promotes my books for free. In addition, they handle all of fulfilments that I cannot afford to do it myself. If I have to handle more than 100 orders a month, I do not have time to enjoy life. So, thanks to Amazon.com.
###

Advice to a friend starting a new business
http://tonyp4idea.blogspot.com/2014/05/starting-music-business.html
One voice

8   Monitor my big gainers

This chapter checks the characteristics of my big winners and the next chapter is on my big losers. The purpose of these two chapters is to demonstrate how to check out the common characteristics of the winners and losers in addition to what strategies work and what do not work in the recent market.

Once the common characteristics of our big winners have been identified, search stocks with the same characteristics. It does not always guarantee the same result. However, it would increase your trading profits more often than not.

In my system of evaluating stocks, it consists of two major parts:

1. Screen for stocks (same as search).
2. Analyze the screened stocks (scoring them to start with).

The database
The following data accounts for all the portfolio holdings and the stocks I sold this year in my largest taxable account as of 6/1/2013. My trading strategy keeps track of a lot of stocks, about 50 in this account. This monitor includes 21 stocks (CSCO bought two times), which had a greater than 25% return. The result is too small to draw a concrete conclusion. However, the result of this monitoring is quite compatible with the results of the previous monitors.

To increase your database, consider the following:

- Include the stocks that you have evaluated even if they have not been bought. Highly recommended.
- Include the entire year of sold stocks not only YTD.
- Relax your threshold of the big gainers (use 20% instead of 25%).
- Include all accounts. I skip some accounts as they serve different purposes such as one for a momentum strategy.

The results
The results are summarized by the following four tables:

Performance
It is a rising market. It should be compared to a market index.

Table 1: Performance Summary.

No.	Avg. Return	Avg. Annualized	Avg. Holding Period
21	50%	111%	211 days

Source

Table 2: Source of the stocks:

Sources	Web & media	Deeply valued	Acquire candidate	Misc. screens	Short squeeze
No.	4	3	3	10	1
Annual. Return	75%	53%	204%	115%	164%
Stocks	ADM, BSX, C, EMN	CSCO, CSCO, MSFT	CAMP, FFCH, ADES	ACAT,BIIB CUZ,DGI,NSIT, STRZA,USNA, OMX,DLTR	DECK

The returns are annualized for a better comparison.

Web and Publication.
There are four (from a total of 21) stocks are selected from articles off from the web, magazines and newspaper. When I was convinced that there was great appreciation potential, I bought that stock without further evaluation (not recommended). I was lazy but you should do some evaluation. Need to distinguish whether the authors are pumping-and-dumping the stocks they recommended.

Deeply-valued stocks.
Three of the stocks were quite deeply valued. I placed an order with prices about 5% lower than the market prices betting they are still on its way down a little. About three out of six orders were successfully executed. If I have a time machine, I should place market orders on all six as the market is rising. Try to buy all the deeply-valued stocks in the future.

I doubled my normal bet on most of these stocks (CSCO about 4 times). As of 5/2013, these deeply-valued stocks have not realized its potential values and they're the under-performers in the group. However, the average 53% annualized return is nothing to sneeze at!

Update 3/2016. Both CSCO and MSFT have been doing great. From 5/1/2013 to 3/1/2016, their average annualized return is 16% vs SPY's 9%.

Candidates to be acquired.

There are quite a few candidates that would be acquired by other (usually larger) companies in the early recovery of the market cycle (a phase defined by me). However, with plenty of easy money around due to low interest rates and the high corporate cash reserves, it extends the acquisition craze to 2013. This phase will end when the Fed begins to tighten the money supply. These stocks represent the better return from the group and I should have doubled bet on all of them even though they normally are smaller and unknown companies.

The potential candidates to be acquired are usually smaller companies with a technological edge and/or having a valuable customer base. Sell them when they're no longer candidates.

Miscellaneous screens.

A screen consists of criteria in searching stocks such as P/E < 20. There are 10 stocks from miscellaneous screens (same as searches). The performance of each screen is further analyzed. It is better to use the screens that have had better performances most recently. My screens are different from yours and some require subscription services, so they will not be disclosed here.

Short squeeze.

The short squeeze happens when the stocks that have been over-sold by the shorters. When the stock is over-sold , those seeking a short position cannot find the extra shares lent to be shorted and sometimes the shorters are forced to cover their shorts due to the high expenses of shorting that stock (interests and dividends).

If the company is not heading towards bankruptcy, any good news would also boost the stock price. This is the typical situation, but it does not work all of the time with TSLA as recent example as of 5/2013. However, I bet TSLA will fall again from its unjustified high price of over $170 per share. Only time can tell.

Increase bets on stocks that have better appreciation potential

The confidence in my predictions for CSCO's future is so secure that I have bought it four times, and then 2 times for BSX and STRZA. All scored high in my scoring system.

Table 3: Score (using the score system in my book Scoring Stocks:

Avg. Score	Foreign Country	Insider Purchase
3.00	0	1

The average score of 9 stocks is 3 and that is the passing grade in my scoring system. The stocks that have not been scored usually have good appreciation potential, deeply-valued from first impression, and / or recommended by convincing articles. The scoring system is a guide line and we do not have to follow it religiously.

There is not a single foreign stock in this group. I usually do not trust the financial statements of the smaller, foreign countries. The next chapter may convince you to skip most of them at least for now or until it is proven otherwise.

Only one stock has meaningful insiders' purchases out of 21. The data base is too small for any conclusion. From my past data, Insiders' Purchases with purchase prices close to the market prices is a good predictor.

By Sectors

Table 4: Sectors:

Sector	Tech	Health Care, equip & drug	Consumer goods	Finance	Retail	Misc.
No.	6	4	3	3	2	3
Ann.	77%	230%	102%	60%	57%	78%
Stock	CAMP CSCO, CSCO, DGI, MSFT NSIT	BIIB, BSX, USNA, ADES	ACAT, ADM DECK	C,FFCH, BANR	OMX, DLTR	CUZ, STRZA, EMN

Technology companies.
Technology companies are doing fine but they are also included in the worst performers described in the next chapter. I rate it a neutral. Just buy the tech companies with high scores and good outlooks for the company and its sector. In general, tech is doing well in a rising market as consumers have more money for high tech toys and companies have money to invest such as upgrading their accounting software.

Mining companies.
Miners are not doing so well in this period as described in the next chapter. Monitor this sector as they may be rotated back in when the economy improves with higher demands for industrial ores. There is no miner in the winners' circle.

Health care, medical equipment and drugs.
With the aging population, the companies in health care, drugs (generic preferred), and medical equipment should be doing great. It is the best performing sector.

The last 90-day performances of ETFs specified in sectors are better predictors for sectors.

Conclusion

The data base of 50 stocks is too small to make any conclusion. However, this result is pretty compatible with the previous monitor about 6 months ago and a large database (with about 200 stocks) that includes stocks that have been evaluated but not bought over the last year.

Personal performance monitor

I have more sophisticated ways and better tools to monitor performance. Most of them require subscriptions (though most of them are low cost), so it will not do the average reader any good to describe them here. They are briefly described as follows.

1. Searches. I have the name of the screens with their average returns. Currently I have about 20 screens I use to search for stocks.

2. Evaluate stocks. Each screened stock should be scored and the performance after 3 months should be compared to S&P500 or its corresponding index such as tech stocks to QQQ. The prediction for the accuracy of each fundamental metric should be checked periodically.

In addition, I divide the data base into short term (about 6 months) and long term (about 12 months). For taxable accounts, you may want to buy stocks in taxable accounts to take advantage of the lower capital tax on long-term gains – check current tax law.

Afterthoughts

- Health care sector. Click here for a SA article.
  (http://seekingalpha.com/article/1503232-bull-of-the-day-biogen)

- We need to check how the portfolio performs when the market goes down. The best performance is when it beats the market in both market directions. However, there is no evergreen strategy. You should use a strategy that is supposed to be favorable in specific market conditions.

Links

Selling short:
http://en.wikipedia.org/wiki/Sell_short
Short squeeze:
http://en.wikipedia.org/wiki/Short_squeeze
Over-sold:
http://www.investopedia.com/terms/o/oversold.asp

9   Monitor my big losses

This chapter is a repeat of the last chapter except with my big losers. It is more important to learn from big losers so we will not buy the 167potential losers if they fit into a certain pattern. You may benefit more from my mistakes or what have been identified as not working in the current market conditions.

The database

The database is smaller due to the current rising market. Partly, it is due to my avoiding the potential losers from previous monitors.

I delete the stocks which have less than a 25% loss. It only has 11 stocks from a total of about 50. A database of 11 stocks is too small to draw any conclusions. However, the results are compatible with previous results. In another words, they follow similar patterns.

The results

As in the last chapter, the results are summarized by the following four tables:

Table 1: Performance Summary.

No.	Avg. Return	Avg. Annualized	Avg. Holding period
11	-43%	-163%	223 days

From here on, annualized returns will be used.

Table 2: Source of the stocks:

Sources	Deeply valued	Acquire candidates	Misc. screens	Short squeezed
No.	0	0	11	0
Annualized Return			-163%	
Stocks			BPI,NTE, SIGA,SIM, VELT,STEC, IAG, END,DEER, CRUS,HXM	

All the stocks here were from my screens. I still find the screens with better recent performances still perform better than the average.

There is not a single stock from the categories of web & publication, deeply-valued list, being acquired or being short squeezed that we find in the last chapter.

Table 3: Score (using the score system):

Avg. Score	Foreign Country
1.86	6
Annualized	-216%

The average score is 1.86 (3 is a passing grade defined in my book Scoring Stocks). Four (out of 11) stocks have not been scored. If I scored them, I may not buy them.

There is not a single stock with a meaningful insider purchase. I have encountered that the lowly-scored stocks with meaningful insider purchases appreciate more than the average. Most foreign companies do not have to list insider information.

There are too many foreign stocks in this group (not a single foreign stock among the best performers as described in the last chapter). I usually do not trust the financial statements of the smaller, emerging countries. If I skipped these six stocks, I would have saved a bundle. We cannot go back in time, but it is a strong guide for the future. I do not know why I still bought foreign stocks as they did not perform well in the last monitoring period.

Luckily I did not place any double bets on any of these losers.

Table 4: Sectors:

Sector	Tech	Miner	Health care, equip and drug	Misc.
No.	4	3	1	2
Annual. Return	-128%	-131%	-34%	-734%
Stocks	NTE,VELT, STEC,CRUS	SIM,IAG END	SIGA	BPI,HXM

Miners are not doing well in this period. Watch out for this sector as it flows with the global economy. Most miners are foreign companies. I do trust their financial data except from Canada and Australia.

Technology companies are not doing so well. However, we have some technology companies included as the top performers as described in the last chapter. The only difference is most of the losers are smaller companies and most are foreign companies. I rate Tech a neutral. Buy those tech companies with high scores and good outlooks.

Performance

The combined annualized return of my big losers is 73%. It should be far higher as I placed multiple purchases on many winners (four times on CSCO and two times on BSX, DGI and STRZA) and none for the losers.

Update I did another performance analysis in 1/2015 including all the stocks that had been screened but I had not bought. Except one from 25 stocks, they are either lowly scored, foreign companies and/or miners. Nine stocks had a grade of F from Blue Chip Growth. Surprisingly six of them had heavy insider purchases.

Conclusion

The data base of 11 stocks is too small to draw a conclusion. However, the conclusion of this monitoring is very similar to the one I did with the larger database of about 200 stocks (vs. 50 stocks this time) 6 months ago.

In combining the results of the two chapters, my conclusions are:
1. The stocks with high scores perform better than those with low scores on the average.

2. Screens (searches) are monitored separately with about a total of 200 stocks and from about 20 screens. Buying candidates that are acquisition prospects have been profitable for this year and 2003.

3. From this monitor and the previous, foreign companies including those companies listed in the U.S. exchanges under perform the USA market.

4. Miners do not perform this time. It could be due to the so-called sector rotation. When the economy improves or this sector is recognized as being over-sold, most industrial metals would return to the former price levels.

5. The better performances from sector health care, medical equipment, or drugs... are responding to the aging population.

6. My previous monitors had identified that foreign companies did not perform on the average. I still have several foreign companies this time. If I had omitted them, the return of this portfolio should be far better. I need to follow my recent results.

7. I bet less on the risky companies (most were small companies and /or had low scores) and bet more on better companies. It is profitable to bet on stocks that have higher appreciation potential.

8. Read articles on this topic. Here is <u>one</u>.

#Filler: An interview of a successful fund manager
This is a typical interview of fund managers that I read in magazines. Learn from what are applicable to us and ignore most ideas that do not make sense. Let me argue for and against them. The name is withdrawn to protect the innocent.

1. "Never can predict market crashes". Look at my simple chart that has successfully detected the two crashes since 2000.
2. "No. 1 in last 10 years, but lags the market in the last 5 years". The last five years is more important to his investors. It could also be due to his asset has grown more than 15 times. Another bad sign for his future performance.
3. "Seldom sell". Most stocks change a lot in 3 years. Portfolio churning improves the quality of a portfolio. I prefer one turn over a year.
4. "Visiting many companies". It is not applicable to our retail investors. I also hear many stories that the officers set up a good show to fool the analysts. We can look at the financial sheets that cannot lie easily and legally for a long period of time.
5. "Water is a long-term trend". Yes, it is. However, I have bad experience in using this idea too early.

6. He continued to show how some of his stocks made over 100%. Let you be reminded that he did not beat the market in the last five years. Hence, he was not being kind enough to show his losers which may be more important than learning from his gainers.

10   Year-end strategies

I have two: 1. Buy the current year winners (YEW) and 2. Buy the current year losers (YEL).

The first strategy is riding the institutional investors' window dressing to include the winners in their funds to make them look better.

The second strategy takes advantage of selling losers for tax purposes. We need to find value stocks, not stocks that are heading to bankruptcy.

The following describes how to create your own testing if you have a historical database. It would be a frame of testing other strategies.

- Define the starting date. For the first strategy, I would use 10/1 and 11/1 for two sets of test. For the second strategy, I would use 12/1 and 12/15. Check which starting date is better for the specific strategy.
- Define the durations, the number of months before you sell the bought stocks. I use 2 months, 4 months, 6 months and 12 months for the durations.
- Define the numbers of tests. I start from 2000, one or two years older if your historical database allows. However, do not use dates older than 1995 as the market was quite different then.
- Compare your results to SPY (or the S&P 500 index).
- Ignore dividends for simplicity.
- Use annualized rates for better comparison.
- If the date has no data such as holidays and weekends, use the date after it for consistency.
- Take out stocks that would not be the stocks you usually buy, penny stocks (that likely boost the performance due to survivorship bias), small foreign companies and/or stocks giving huge dividends or giving return of capital.
- Use different metric to sort, such as Expected Earning Yield (E/P) or a composite grade. Use the top 10 (or 5) stocks.

- Include maximum drawback (the maximum loss) from many selected durations. My maximum loss is -52% from 12/1/2007 to one year later in my Year-End Loss strategy, but followed by 256% gain in the next year.
- Negative percent numbers could give wrong calculations comparing to the index. Check them out manually if your formula has not taken care of the negative numbers.
- Here are my best results for the two strategies. Again, my results will not be the same as yours due to different selections. Past performances may have nothing to do with future performances.

The year-end loser strategy in 2015 does not work that well as I screened many stocks that are scored very low. I found out many screened stocks are foreign countries. Many emerging countries have problems and I do not trust most of their financial info. Besides that, many are energy companies that I already have too many.

Many have Expected Earning Yields over 35%. However, most have very high debts such as Debt/Equity is over 1 (i.e. 100%). If I bought them, I would unload them in 3 months fearing a market crash in 2016. Historically, it is profitable, but I may skip most YEL stocks this year as most are deserved losers. The lesson is: Adjust to the current market conditions.

Strategy	Starting Date	Duration	Avg. Annual. %	Max. Drawn Down
YE Winners	10/1	4 months	40%	-36%
YE Losers	12/1	6 months	42%	-28%

My experience

Making good money needs to find a strategy that matches to the current market. Here are my recent strategies I actually tried with money in 2018.
* Window dressing for institutional investors from Nov. 1 to Dec. 1 (some use dates earlier than Nov. 1). Buy current winners and sell current losers of stocks with large market cap.

The market was risky so I did not buy winners but shorted some losers.

* Buy year-end losers from Nov. 1 to Dec. 31 (some use dates earlier than Nov.1). The companies have to be profitable (>15%), big losers (most having over 50% yearly loss) and small companies (preferred).

Incorporate the strategy with today's volatile market (i.e. buy when they plunge and sell when they rise). Determine what is "plunge" and "rise". For me, it is short-term and the percent is 5% from recent high or low.

There is a selling part of these strategies I have not included here. Most of my strategies are based on exhaustive tests from historical data with a lot of work.

Every market is different. We need to make a lot of adjustments. From my experiences, the best research may not make you money all the time. In the long run, the more educated your work, the better chance of making money.

Year-End 2018

This is one of my best monthly returns. The average purchase date is 12/27/2018 and the current prices were based on 1/28/2019. The return is 53% and 648% annualized. Most likely the performance will not be repeated. However, it serves as a procedure for coming years.

I change the quantity Q to 1. Several stocks have been purchased more than once. Sold 3 stocks already with Status = 'Sold'.

Account	Screen	Year-end loser		Start	12/21/19	End	1/8/2019	Today	1/28/19	
Stock	Q	Buy	Sell	Buy $	Sell $	Buy Date	Sell Date	# Days	Profit $	Profit %	Ann %	Status
401KC											
CHK	1	2.13	2.99	2	3	01/03/19	01/18/19	15	1	40%	982%	Sold
MNK	1	16.41	21.45	16	21	01/03/19	01/25/19	22	5	31%	510%	Sold
MNK	1	16.43	21.45	16	21	01/03/19	01/25/19	22	5	31%	507%	Sold
NNBR	1	5.68	8.58	6	9	12/26/18	01/28/19	33	3	51%	565%	
NNBR	1	5.72	8.58	6	9	12/26/18	01/28/19	33	3	66%	727%	
ESTE	1	4.35	6.45	4	6	12/26/18	01/18/19	23	2	48%	766%	Sold
JT											
LCI	1	4.61	8.29	5	8	12/21/18	01/28/19	38	4	80%	767%	
MDR	1	8.01	9.13	8	9	01/08/19	01/28/19	20	1	14%	255%	
YRCW	1	3.29	5.78	3	6	12/21/18	01/28/19	38	2	76%	727%	
YRCW	1	3.26	5.78	3	6	12/21/18	01/28/19	38	3	77%	742%	
401K											
ASRT	1	3.56	4.18	4	4	12/26/18	01/28/19	33	1	17%	193%	
UTCC	1	7.13	11.00	7	11	12/26/18	01/28/19	33	4	54%	600%	
YRCW	1	2.92	5.78	3	6	12/26/18	01/28/19	33	3	98%	1083%	
Tot/avg				84	119	12/27/18		29	36	53%	648%	

I sold my YRCW (not shown above) on the earnings date that can be found in Finviz.com. It is a mistake. If the earnings are positive, it will be sold for my asking price plus a little more but less than the surge. If it is negative, it will not be sold. Recommend to cancel the sell order before the earnings date.

As of 09/07/2019, LCI is up by 185% and YRCW is down by 27% (I sold one position in my retirement account for about 100% gain).

How long should we hold these screened stocks?

Except those in taxable account, I sold all of them in the first two months. The following is the annualized returns for holding 1 month, 2 months, 3 months and 5 months (as of 6/22/2019). From my previous testing, I should hold the stocks for 6 months. However, I have made my objective already and I want to take advantage of this volatile market.

I could not find UTCC in my historical database. I sold it with an annualized return of 572%. It could be acquired or merged. For simplicity, I used 12/27/2018 as the purchase dates for all stocks. I consider one position for each stock and hence 3 purchases of YRCW is considered at one purchase. Again, I do not include dividends, the bid spread and commissions.

	1 Month	2 Months	3 Months	5 Months
Ann. Return	497%	366%	178%	17%
SPY	72%	74%	52%	31%

From the above, I did well in selling most of them. If I held all of them for 5 months, they would not beat the SPY, the market to many.

Fillers

- First bought or sold by insiders and their relatives, then followed by programmed computers, institutional investors, technicians and retail investors.
- Missed to short PG&E and VALE when the news broke. There is more in life than playing the market.
- The shutdown costs more than enough to build Trump's Great Wall of America. How stupid the politicians can be? How stupid are the voters? Do not vote for the politicians who use shutdown as a tool!!!

11   Tom's conservative strategy

The following is a summary of Tom's conservative strategy as described in his profile on Seeking Alpha website. Use it as an example and modify it to fit your investing philosophy. You need to ignore your friends telling you how much money he is making when the market is up. You also need not tell them how much money you're not losing, otherwise you will not have any friends.

Click here (for Kindle readers) for Tom's strategy.
(http://tonyp4idea.blogspot.com/2012/05/tom-armisteads-investment-strategy.html)

Ignore the date posted as this is one of the very few strategies that are evergreen. As of 12/2015, it does not perform well during 2009 (or 2010) to 2015 due to the long, unexpected rising market. However, it beats the above two strategies by good margins in the long run.

A winning strategy for couch potatoes

My friend John has a very similar strategy similar to Tom's. My friend is making money with the least risk. He only buys stocks after the market crashes and sell stocks when the market rises. Ignore all market pundits. This is recommended to anyone who does not have time to monitor his/her investment.

He bought stocks in 2008-2010 and sold them after 2010. It was very profitable for him in 2000-2008 using this simple strategy. However, he missed the gains from 2010 to 2018. It is unusual that we have such a long bull market. I beg he is still beating most mutual fund managers with this simple strategy that does not require much work.

Enhance a good strategy

Following the favorable stages to trade in the market cycle described in this book:
- Buy SPY in the Early Recovery phase (about 1 ½ year after the crash or use the entry point described in Market Timing in this book.
- Sell SPY in one or two years after the buy.

Here are some options if you have time to watch the market.

- Buy stocks (or an ETF that simulates the market) in Nov. 1 and sell them in May 1. I prefer to buy stocks on Oct. 15 and sell them on April 15 to avoid the herd.
- Buy stocks on Dec. 1 and sell them on Feb. 1 to take advantage of the best (statistically) period of the year.
- Buy stocks in the year before the election and sell them after a year.
- Add long-term bonds when the interest rates is high (say more than 5%). Switch to short-term bonds or cash when the interest rate is low (say less than 2%).
- If you have time, time the market by following my simple technique to exit and reenter the market.

Spend the rest of the time on your comfortable couch (i.e. enjoying life) or sip some fancy tropical drink served by some beautiful tropical lady on some nice tropical island. Not a bad strategy! Of course, the market is not always rational and there is always risk involved.

An alternative to Tom's strategy

Have a list of value stocks to buy and update the list periodically (say every 3 months).

When the market loses 5%, buy them at 2% less than the market prices or alternatively 5% less than the prices on your list.

Decide when to sell such as making 12% profit or losing 12%. If the market is not risky, you may want to keep them longer. It should work in a sideways market but not during market plunges.

John's Strategy

John maintains about 75% cash and only buys blue chip stocks at 52-week low. He ignores friends telling him about making good money when the market is up.

Here are my changes for better returns at the expense of taking more risk. I would maintain 50% cash and 0% in Early Recovery, a phase in the market cycle defined by me. I would also include all stocks with market cap over 1 billion and stocks close to 5% of their bottoms. In addition, I would evaluate the stocks before I buy as some stocks may go to zero.

12   Top-down investing

The nutshell is described here. Only buy stocks when the market is favorable. Find the best industry (a subsector) and then find the best stock(s) within the selected industry. In doing so, our chances of successful investing are substantially increased.

It is so simple and it has been proven by many including myself. I just wonder why it has not been extensively practiced. I offer a simple trade plan as follows:

1. Do not invest when the market is plunging. I have a simple way to detect market plunges without any expensive subscriptions or tools.

2. Select the best industry (most are represented by an ETF or ETFs specific for the industry or sector). For example, Technology is a sector. Computer and Software are industries (subsector under Technology). From time to time I use sectors for simplicity and most free sites do not sub divide the sectors into industries. Check out the best-performing industry or sector from last month in many sites including SeekingAlpha and CNNfn.

   If you're a value investor, you may not want to choose the timeliest sector but the most under-valued sector. Value investors should hold the sectors/stocks longer (such as 6 months or even longer) for the market to recognize their values.

   In addition, you need to detect the sector/stock rotation by the institutional investors who control over 75% of all trades (i.e. smart money). They will rotate sector/stock when they find better profit potential in another sector/stock. Use stops to prevent further losses.

   If you do not have time to research on stocks, trade ETFs for sectors and skip the next step.

3. The final step is to select the best stock(s) within the sector via fundamental analysis (including intangible analysis), insider trading analysis, institution trading analysis and technical analysis.

   Do not let these terms scare you. We will start with the simplest approach without any subscription and a lot of effort.

4. The next step is when to reevaluate and sell the stocks when conditions change or they meet your objectives. If the market is plunging, sell all stocks.

Stick with and repeat the entire process.

The easiest retirement planning system

Have a budget and live within your means. Buy good stuff that lasts for a long time. After saving enough cash for emergency and planned expenses such as vacation, new car, college, etc., invest your extra money in a retirement account (Roth IRA if allowable) with 80% in a market ETF and 20% in a short-term bond ETF.

Run the chart described in the market cycle chapters once a month. If the chart tells you to exit the market, move all to cash. Reenter the market when the chart tells you to do so. It beats most if not all of your financial plans from the best experts money can buy.

Afterthoughts

My late friend had a 'buy and hold strategy' that worked pretty well. Most of his stocks were big companies. He died with a house worth more than a million and many millions in stocks. His only mistake was not to transfer more of his stocks to his heirs before his death. He died on the year when the estate exemption returned back to a million. Uncle Sam was the biggest winner and won big without any effort.

Epilogue

Some Chinese words have no straight-forward English translations or equivalents and here is one. We have the mutual privileges to connect to each other via this book. We call it 'Yuen' in Chinese or 'fate' in very, very rough translation.

English is not my native language and investing is not my career which is IT. I have never taken any class in economics, accounting, business and investing except those required in my Industrial Engineering degrees. Hence, writing a book on investing is quite remote.

After my early retirement, I have been spending most of my time in investing, running thousands of simulation and reading over one hundred books in investing. Starting from 2000, I have been doing extraordinarily good. I comment in financial blogs and save the good ones in my own blog, so I can refer them later on. After several years, I have enough information to write a book.

Shamelessly I use many public websites to promote my book. My mission is different. I use it to help my fellow investors to be a better investor. The income from this book and the articles provides me less than 1% of my income so far.

It is far more financially rewarding working on my investment including finding new strategies. Writing books and articles takes time away from my investing and it actually costs me more money. However, it has been fun to write this book and to interact with my readers. Money cannot buy everything and the satisfaction of holding a printed book with my 'ugly' picture on the book cover.

I do not believe that this book or any book is the Holy Grail in investing. However, it has a lot of fresh ideas and good pointers that have bought me financial success (at least so far). I ask my readers to challenge my pointers and ensure they are applicable in today's market and meet their objectives and requirements.

A good pointer can make you thousands of dollars, and a bad or misinterpreted one can do the opposite. Always do paper trading on any strategy and / or idea before you commit real money on it. Start your strategy with cash in small increments until you have more confidence.

Hopefully, this book's primary objective enabling you to be a better investor is met. Actually, you should be a better investor than I am if you can integrate your knowledge you already have with mine – I called it adding wings to a roaring tiger.

This book should be read repeatedly to remind us (I am a reader too) of any error(s) we repeated. Some chapters are not easy to read as this book is not intended to be so. You need to practice what it suggests such as learning how to detect market plunge. In any case, try out any strategy with paper trading before committing real money gradually and slowly.

There are many styles in investing. It is better to master one at a time than trying to master several. Personally I select swing trading with 6 months to renew my investment. Sector Rotation and momentum trading are my other styles I practice.

I made a lot of predictions. I have more rights than wrongs compared to most authors. I never use after-the-fact for predictions. Even the predictions are wrong, use the logics behind.

The advantages of self-publishing of eBooks are low prices to you, frequently updated...

If you order the printed of this book from Amazon.com, check whether you are eligible for a free or at low cost for the Kindle version that has all the clickable links. The Art of Investing should be your next book. Be warned that many chapters here are copied from the Art of Investing.

A link is provided for future updates and announcements.
https://ebmyth.blogspot.com/2020/01/updates.html

My blog:
https://tonyp4idea.blogspot.com/

Final notes

Thanks for reading this book and I hope it will be beneficial to your financial health. If so, comment on it on Amazon.com or the place you bought this book. I will be very grateful.

I believe the readers are getting a very good deal in reading this book. To benefit more, you have to try out the techniques described in this book and paper trade them thoroughly until you are successful.

I have put everything I know on investing in this lengthy book. I do not expect you to buy another of my books if it is over 250 pages long as they will have many duplicated chapters. However, the following book has recommended stocks: "Best Stocks to buy in 2020".

I had 50% in a month return in the 2018-year end using year-end strategy and many good picks before. It will include less than 20 books for better picks. A very popular book in 2019 recommending 100 stocks did not even beat the market.

Appendix 1 – All my books

- <u>Art</u> of Investing (highly recommended combining most of my books on investing). It has over 500 pages (6*9), double the size of an average investing book. Similar books: Using <u>Fidelity</u>. Using <u>Finviz</u>.
- Sector <u>Rotation: 21 Strategies</u> and <u>Shorting Stocks and ETFs</u> have more specific chapters on the topic.
- Using Profitable <u>Investing Sites</u>. <u>Investing Lessons</u>.
- <u>Best stocks</u> for 2022.
- "Nuclear <u>War</u> with China?"
- Books for today's market: Profit from Coming Market <u>Crash</u>.
- The following books are in a series: <u>Finding</u> Profitable Stocks, <u>Market</u> Timing and <u>Scoring</u> Stocks.
- Books on strategies: <u>Trading System</u>, <u>Swing (Rotation + Momentum)</u>, <u>ETF Rotation</u> for Couch Potatoes, <u>Momentum</u>, <u>SuperStocks</u>, <u>Dividend</u>, <u>Penny & Micro</u> Stock, and <u>Retiree</u>.
- Books for advance beginners: <u>Be an expert</u> (highly recommended), <u>Introduce</u>, Investing for <u>Beginners</u>, <u>Beat</u> Fund Managers, Profit via <u>ETFs</u>, <u>Buffett</u>, <u>Ideas</u>, <u>Conservative</u> and <u>Top-Down</u>.
- Miscellaneous: Investing <u>Strategies</u>. Buy <u>Low</u> and Sell High. Buy <u>High</u> and sell Higher. <u>Buffettology</u>. <u>Technical Analysis</u>. <u>Trading</u> Stocks.
- Concise Editions and Introduction Editions are available at very low prices and are competitive with books of similar sizes (50 pages) and prices ($3 range).

Most books have paperbacks. Links and offers are subject to change without notice.

Best stocks to buy for 2022

We care about performance only. Not considering dividends and fees, my last three books in this series have beaten the SPY (the market to most) by **110%, 71% and 25%** from the publish date to 07/01/2021. Next book could be on 12/15/2022

Book	Stocks	Return	Ann.	Beat SPY by
Best Book for 2021 2nd Edition	10	20%	52%	110%
Best Book for 2021	4	29%	52%	71%
Best Book to Buy from Aug, 2020	14	42%	45%	25%
Avg.	9	31%	50%	69%

Sector Rotation: 21 Strategies

- On 5/26/2020, I searched for "Sector Rotation" under Amazon's Book. They are listed in the same order except my book Sector Rotation: 21 Strategies.

Book	Date	Size[1]	Kindle $[1]	Hard $
Sector Rotation: 21 Strategies	**05/2020**	**425**	**$9.95**	$24.95
Super Sectors	09/2010	289	$26.39	$49.95
Dual Momentum Investing	11/2014	240	$40.40	$42.20
Sector Investing	05/1996	260		$29.94
Sector Trading Strategies	08/2007	164	$26.39	$16.66
The Sector Strategist	03/2012	225	$26.39	$44.96
ETF Rotation	10/2012	125	**$9.95**	**$14.99**
Optimal... Sector Rotation	07/2015	80		$44.07

[1] From Amazon on size and prices as of 5/25/2020.

My book won in all categories except the price for hard copy in one. However, my book won as the lowest cost per page by a wide margin. In addition, as of 5/2020 I bet that no author besides me made over 4 times using sector rotation starting the amount more than his yearly salary then.

- I have **21** strategies in sector rotation while most books have only one. It ranges from simple rotation of a stock ETF and cash for beginners to many advanced strategies for experts. Most other books have one or two strategies.

- Andrew, a contributor on Sector Rotation article at Seeking Alpha, said, "Great stuff, Tony. It's great to meet experienced traders such as yourself. I had a browse through the book and think your method is a little more refined than mine."

- "You have written the book in a way that makes good and logical sense." Bill.

- Do not be fooled by past performances. Just check the recent performance of the top 50 stocks selected by IBD in the last five years. The mediocre result (hopefully it will change) could be due to too many followers and/or there is no evergreen strategy. I seldom heard the fantastic results from the followers of O'Neil, our greatest chartist. The adaptive strategy of this book shows you how to select the most profitable strategy for the current market.

- I switched most (if not all) my sector funds in April, 2000 from technology sectors to traditional sectors (better to money market fund). We can reduce losses by spotting market plunges and the sector trend.

Shorting Stocks and ETFs

Recent performances.

Stocks	Short Date	Close date	Duration	Return	Annualized
ACVA	06/10/21	09/29/21	111	22%	72%
CCL	07/14/21	09/29/21	77	-8%	-36%
CENX	09/17/21	09/29/21	12	3%	105%
CLOV	09/16/21	09/29/21	13	10%	291%
CSPR	09/16/21	09/29/21	13	33%	917%
EOSE	09/15/21	09/29/21	14	10%	261%
MILE	07/22/21	09/29/21	69	53%	279%
NCLH	07/27/21	09/29/21	64	-5%	-27%
REAL	06/04/21	09/29/21	117	22%	68%
UAVS	06/04/21	09/29/21	117	41%	127%
Average	07/30/21	09/29/21	61	18%	206%
RSP	S&P 500			0%	

It is for education purposes and I am not responsible for any errors. As in most parts of this book, commissions, dividends and fees (interest for shorts) are not included, and hence the returns are less than specified. They are real and all trades for the period.

Stocks	Short Date	Close date	Duration	Return	Annualized
BBIG[1]	09/30/21	11/19/21[1]	50	35%	258%
BFLY	09/30/21	11/18/21	49	14%	107%
EOLS	11/10/21	11/17/21	7	10%	523%
FLDM	10/13/21	11/18/21	36	14%	147%
MKFG	10/27/21	11/18/21	22	-9%	-149%
PAVM[1]	10/20/21	11/19/21[1]	30	34%	413%
TSP	10/05/21	11/18/21	44	-11%	-91%
VRM	10/13/21	11/17/21	35	13%	135%
Average	10/14/21	11/18/21	34	13%	168%
RSP	S&P 500			4%	

Appendix 2 – Art of Investing

Art of Investing consisting of 15 books in 1. Besides saving money and your digital shelve space, it gives you quick reference and concentration on the topic you're currently interested in. It covers most investing topics in investing excluding speculative investing such as currency trading and day trading. It has over 500 pages (6*9), about the size of two investing books of average size.

The 15 books

Book No.	Amazon.com
1	Simple techniques
2	Finding Stocks
3	Evaluating Stocks
4	Scoring Stocks
5	Trading Stocks
6	Market Timing
7	Strategies
8	Sector Rotation
9	Insider Trading
10	Penny Stocks & Micro Cap
11	Momentum Investing
12	Dividend Investing
13	Technical Analysis
14	Investing Ideas
15	Buffettology

The book links are subject to change without notice.

"How to be a billionaire" is for beginners and couch potatoes, who can use the advanced features of this book in the simplest and less time-consuming techniques. Most advance users can skip this section unless they want to use some of the short cuts described.

We start with the basic books Finding Stocks, Evaluate Stocks, Trading Stocks and Market Timing. You can select and start with one of the many styles and strategies in investing such as swing trading and top-down strategy. Many tools are described in other books such as ETFs, technical analysis, covered calls and trading plan.

Many books start with "Why" to lure you to read more and are followed by "How" and then the theory behind the book.
If the book you're reading is beneficial to you, imagine how it would with 850 pages.

Most readers' comments are on "Debunk the Myths in Investing", which this book is originally based on. As of 2018, I did not know any of the commentators on my books.

"I skipped ahead to his chapter book 14 (of "Complete the Art of Investing"), Investment Advice just to get a feel of his writing style. His research is phenomenal and doesn't overwhelm with big words or catchy "sales-like" tactics.

I truly believe this ordinary man, Mr. Tony Pow, has a gift of explaining his experience as an investor without the bull crap of trying to make you buy his stuff. He seemingly just wants to share his knowledge, tips, and clarity of definitions for the kind of folks like me who want to understand something FIRST before jumping in with emotions of trying to make a boat load of money. I like the technical analysis side he brings.

Mr. Tony Pow talks about hidden gems in his book; well....quite frankly, he is a hidden gem. Thank you and I will also post my comments about this author to my Facebook page!" – JB on this book.

"Excellent book, recommend to all investors... great knowledge. It has fine-tuned my investing strategies... Your book is hard to set aside, as I read it all the time learning good techniques and analysis of stocks, ETF... Since I purchased your book in March, I have underlined, highlighted and placed tabs on top of pages for quick reference." – Aileron on this book.

"Tony, I just finished reading your 2nd edition. It's my pleasure to report that I found it most interesting. You're welcome to use this blurb if you like:

Debunk the Myths in Investing is an all-encompassing look at not only the most salient factors influencing markets and investors, but also a from-the-trenches look at many of the misconceptions and mistakes too many investors make. Reading this book may save not only time and aggravation but money as well!"

Joseph Shaefer, CEO, Stanford Wealth Management LLC.

"Tony, Great work!" from James and Chris, who are portfolio managers.

"'Debunk the Myths in Investing' is a comprehensive book on investing that deals with many aspects of this tense profession in which with a lot of knowledge and a bit of luck (or vice versa) one can greatly benefit...

Therefore 'Debunk the Myths in Investing' is an interesting book that on its 500 pages offer a lot of knowledge related to investing world and many practical advice, so I can recommend its reading if you're interested in this topic."
- Denis Vukosav, Top 500 Reviewers at Amazon.com.

"490 pages (Debunk) of a genius's ranting and hypothesis with various theories throughout, written light-heartedly with ample doses of humor...Yes, the myth of not being able to profitably time the market is BUSTED...

One might ask... Why is he giving away the results of his hard-earned research for only $20? He states that his children are not interested in investing and wants to share his efforts with the world." - Abe Agoda.

"Excellent book, recommend to all investors... great knowledge. It has fine-tuned my investing strategies... Your book is hard to set aside, as I read it all the time learning good techniques and analysis of stocks, ETF... Since I purchased your book in March, I have underlined, highlighted and placed tabs on top of pages for quick reference." - Aileron on this book.

"Great stuff, Tony. It's great to meet experienced traders such as yourself. I had a browse through the book and think your method is a little more refined than mine."
"Your strategy is very rules based and solid. I sometimes envy people who have developed something like this."

Making 50% in one month

I claim to have the best one-month performance ever for recommending 8 or more stocks without using options and leverage. My following return is 57% in a month or 621% annualized. They are slightly different as I calculated the average from the averages of three different accounts. The average buy date is 12/26/18 and the "current date" is 01/28/19.

The performance may not be repeated. I will use the same screen for the coming years and even the expected 10% (or 120% annualized) is very good.

I used the same screen for searching stock candidates. I spent a total of about 20 hours from Dec. 15, 2018 to Jan. 5, 2019.

Stock	Buy Price	Sold or Current Price	Buy date	Sold or Current date	Profit %	Profit % Ann.	Status
CHK	2.13	2.99	01/03/09	01/18/19	40%	982%	Sold
MNK	16.41	21.45	01/03/19	01/25/19	31%	510%	Sold
MNK	16.43	21.45	01/03/19	01/25/19	31%	507%	Sold
NNBR	5.68	8.58	12/26/18	01/28/19	51%	565%	
NNBR	5.72	8.58	12/26/18	01/28/19	66%	727%	
ESTE	4.35	6.45	12/26/18	01/18/19	48%	766%	Sold
LCI	4.61	8.29	12/21/18	01/28/19	80%	767%	
MDR	8.01	9.13	01/08/19	01/28/19	14%	255%	
YRCW	3.29	5.78	12/21/18	01/28/19	76%	727%	
YRCW	3.26	5.78	12/21/18	01/28/19	77%	742%	
ASRT	3.56	4.18	12/26/18	01/28/19	17%	193%	
UTCC	7.13	11.00	12/26/18	01/28/19	54%	600%	
YRCW	2.92	5.78	12/26/18	01/28/19	98%	1083%	

Best one-year return

I claim to have the best-performed article in Seeking Alpha history, an investing site, for recommending 15 or more stocks in one year after the publish date without using options and leverage.

https://seekingalpha.com/article/1095671-amazing-returns-velti-alcatel-lucent-alpha-natural-resources

Your choice for your next book

I was surprised that one told me $25 is a lot for an investing book. It could be less than a taxi cab to the airport attending a seminar, and the time is peanut comparatively.

"Investing Lessons: Successes and Plunders" and "Art of investing 2nd Edition" should be your first choices. If you are short-term trading, I recommend "Sector Rotation: 21 Strategies" and "Shorting Stocks /ETFs 2nd Edition". These books together with "Using Fidelity" and "Using Finviz" share many articles.

A new book every Dec. 15 with a July update (not a promise) is my selections on stocks. So far, the returns of the selected stocks are phenomenal. "A nuclear war with China?" is my views on politics.

Appendix 3 - Our window to the investing world

The paperback version of this chapter can be found in the following link.
http://ebmyth.blogspot.com/2013/11/web-sites.html

- **General**
  Wikipedia / Investopedia /Yahoo!Finance / MarketWatch / Cnnfn / Morningstar /CNBC / Bloomberg / WSJ / Barron's / Motley Fool / TheStreet
- **Evaluate stocks**
  Finviz / SeekingAlpha / MSN Money / Zacks / Daily Finance / ADR / Fidelity / Earnings Impact / OpenInsider / NYSE / NASDAQ / SEC / SEC for 10K and 10Q (quarterly) reports required to file for listed stocks in major exchanges.
- **Charts**
  BigCharts / FreeStockCharts / StockCharts /
- **Screens**
  Yahoo!Finance / Finviz / CNBC / Morningstar /
- **Besides stocks**
  123Jump / Hoover's Online / FINRA Bond Market Data / REIT / Commodity Futures / Option Industry
- **Vendors**

AAII / Zacks / IBD / GuruFocus / VectorVest /
Fidelity / Interactive Brokers / Merrill Lynch /
- **Economy.**
  Econday / EcoconStats / Federal Reserve / Economist /
- **Misc.**
  Dow Jones Indices / Russell / Wilshire /
  IRS / Wikinvest / ETF Database / ETF Trends /
  Nolo (estate planning) / AARP /

Appendix 4 - ETFs / Mutual Funds

What is an ETF

ETFs have basic differences from mutual funds: 1. Lower management expenses, 2. Trade ETFs same as stocks, and 3. Usually more diversified but not more selective than the related mutual funds such as NOBL vs FRDPX.

The major classifications of ETFs are 1. Simulating an index such as SPY, QQQ and DIA, 2. Simulating a sector such as XLE and SOXX, 3. Simulating an asset class such as GLD and SLV, 4. Simulating a country or a group of countries such as EWC and FXI, 5. Managed by a manager(s) such as ARKK, 6. Betting a market or sector to go down such as SH and PSQ, and 7. Leveraged (not recommended for beginners).

Fidelity: Index ETFs (https://www.fidelity.com/etfs/overview).
Wikipedia on ETF (http://en.wikipedia.org/wiki/Exchange-traded_fund).

List of ETFs

ETF database (Recommended): http://etfdb.com/
ETF Bloomberg: http://www.bloomberg.com/markets/etfs/
ETF Trends: http://www.etftrends.com/
A list of ETFs. Seeking Alpha.
http://etf.stock-encyclopedia.com/category/)
A list of contra ETFs (or bear ETFs)
http://www.tradermike.net/inverse-short-etfs-bearish-etf-funds/
Misc.: ETFGuide, ETFReplay
Fidelity low-cost index funds:
https://www.youtube.com/watch?v=zpKi4_IJvlY

Fidelity Annuity funds with performance data.
http://fundresearch.fidelity.com/annuities/category-performance-annual-total-returns-quarterly/FPRAI?refann=005

Other resources
Most subscription services offer research on ETFs. IBD has a strategy dedicated to ETFs and so does AAII to name a couple.

Seeking Alpha has extensive resources for ETF including an ETF screener and investing ideas. So is ETFdb.

Not all ETFs are created equal

Check their performances and their expenses.

When to use or not to use ETFs

I prefer sector mutual funds in some industries, as they have many bad stocks such as drug industry, banks, miners and insurers. Most mutual funds cannot time the market.

When you believe a sector is heading up (or contra ETF for heading down), but you do not have time to do research on specific stocks, buy an ETF for the sector; it is same for the market.

Half ETF

Taking out half of the stocks that score below the average in an index ETF could beat the same full ETF itself. I call it HETF (half the ETF). You heard it here first. To illustrate, sort the expected P/E (not including stocks with negative earnings) in ascending order and only include the stocks on the first half. Add more fundamental metrics. It will take a few minutes.

Disadvantages of ETFs

- When you have two stocks in a sector ETF one good one and one bad one, the ETF treats them the same. Stock pickers would buy the one that has a better appreciation potential.
- Sometimes the return could be misleading due to stock rotation. To illustrate this, on August 29, 2012, SHLD was replaced by LYB in a sector fund. SHLD was down by 4% and LYB was up by 4%

primarily due to the switch. Unless you sell and buy at the right time (which is impossible), your return would not match the ETF's returns due to the replacement.

- Ensure the performance matches the corresponding index; it is hard due to excluding dividends.

Advantages of ETFs

- We have demonstrated that you can beat the market by using market timing. Between 2000 and Nov., 2013, you only exit and reenter the market 3 times and the result is astonishing.
- It is easy to rotate a sector vs. buying/selling all of the stocks in this sector. Rotating a sector is the same as trading a stock.
- The risk is spread out, and your portfolio is diversified especially for a market ETF or buying three or more ETFs in different sectors.
- Periodically the bad stocks in most funds are replaced by better stocks.
- Eliminate the time in researching stocks.

Leveraged ETFs

I do not recommend them. Some are 2x, 3x and even higher. They're too risky for beginners. However, when you are very sure or your tested strategy has very low drawdown, you may want to use them to improve performance. Most leveraged ETFs and contra ETFs have higher fees.

My basic ETF tables

I include some contra ETFs, mutual funds and Fidelity's annuity. Some of these may be interesting to you.

ETFs and funds come and go. Some ideas and classifications are my own interpretation. Refer to ETFdb for updated information. Not responsible for any error. Check out the ETF or fund before you take any action.

Table by market cap:

Category	ETF	Mutual Funds	Fidelity's Annuity	Contra ETF	Alternate
Size:					

Large Cap	DIA	See Blend		DOG	
	SPY			SH	FXAIX VOO
	QQQ			PSQ	FNCMX
	RYH				
Blend	IWD	BEQGX			
Growth	SPYG	FBGRX			FSPGX
Value	SPYV	DOGGX			FLCOX
Dividend	NOBL	FRDPX			
	VYM				
Mid Cap			FNBSC	MYY	
Blend	MDY	VSEQX			
Growth		STDIX			
		BPTRX			
Value		FSMVX			
Small Cap			FPRGC	SBB	FSSNX
Blend	IWM	HDPSX			
Growth		PRDSX			FECGX
Value		SKSEX			FISVX
Micro	IWC				
Multi					
Blend		VDEOX			
Growth		VHCOX			
Value		TCLCX			
Total					FSKAX
Bond					
Long Term (20)	VLV	BTTTX		TBF	
Mid Term (7 – 10)	VCIT	FSTGX			
Short Term (1 – 3 yrs.)	VCSH	THOPX			
Total	BOND	PONDX			
Corp Invest Grade	VCIT	NTHEX			
High Yield (junk)	PHB	SPHIX			
Muni	MUB	Check state			
Special situation					
Buy back	PKW				

Table by sectors:

Sector	ETF	Mutual Funds	Fidelity's Annuity
Banking[1]		FSRBK	
Regional	IAT		
Bio Tech	IBB	FBIOX	
	XBI	Large	
Consumer Dis.	XLY	FSCPX	FVHAC
Consumer Staple	XLP	FDFAX	FCSAC
Finance	KIE	FIDSX	FONNC
	IYF		
Energy	XLE	FSENX	FJLLC
Energy Service		FSESX	
Gold	GLD	FSAGX	
Gold Miner	GDX	VGPMX	
Health Care	IYH	FSPHX	FPDRC
	VHT	VGHCX	
House Builder	ITB	FSHOX	
	ITB	Perform	
Industrial	IYJ	FCYIX	FBALC
Material	VAW	FSDPX	
	IYM		
Oil	USO		
Oil Service	OIH	FSESX	
Oil Exploration	XOP		
Real Estate	VNQ	FRIFX	FFWLC
REIT	VNQ		
Retail	RTH	FSRPX	
	XRT		
Regional bank	KRE	FSRBX	
Semi Conduct	SMH		
Software	XSW	FSCSX	
	IGV		
Technology	XLK	FSPTX	FYENC
	FDN	FBSOX	
		ROGSX	
Telecomm.	VOX	FSTCX	FVTAC
Transport	XTN		

	IYT		
Utilities	XLU	FSUTX	FKMSC
Wireless		FWRLX	

Footnote. [1] Also check Finance.

Table by countries outside the USA:

Country	ETF	Mutual Funds	Fidelity's Annuity	Alternate
Australia	EWA			
Brazil	EWZ			
Canada	EWC	FICDX		
China	FXI	FHKCX		
EAFE	EFA			
Emerging	VWO	FEMEX	FEMAC	FPADX
Europe	VGK	FIEUX		
Global	KXI	PGVFX		
Greece	GREK			
India	INDY	MINDX		
Indonesia	EIDO			
Latin America	ILF	FLATX		
Nordic		FNORX		
Hong Kong	EWH			
Japan	EWJ	FJPNX		
S. Africa	EZA			
S. Korea	EWY	MAKOX		
Singapore	EWS			
Taiwan	EWT			
	TUR			
United Kingdom	EWU			
Foreign:				
Combination				
Intern. Div.	IDV			FTIHX
Small Cap	SCZ			
Value	EFV			
Europe	VGK			

#Filler: Honey, my book can play music.
https://www.youtube.com/watch?v=HxGT5z6d-GA&list=PLMZa6mP7jZ2b1otqG4tfbgZpLEdh6YiNF

It may cut down commercials by casting it to TV.

www.ingramcontent.com/pod-product-compliance
Lightning Source LLC
Chambersburg PA
CBHW070538220526
45467CB00003B/985